Tattoo Flash
Coloring Book

Orginal Artwork
by

Marla Fay

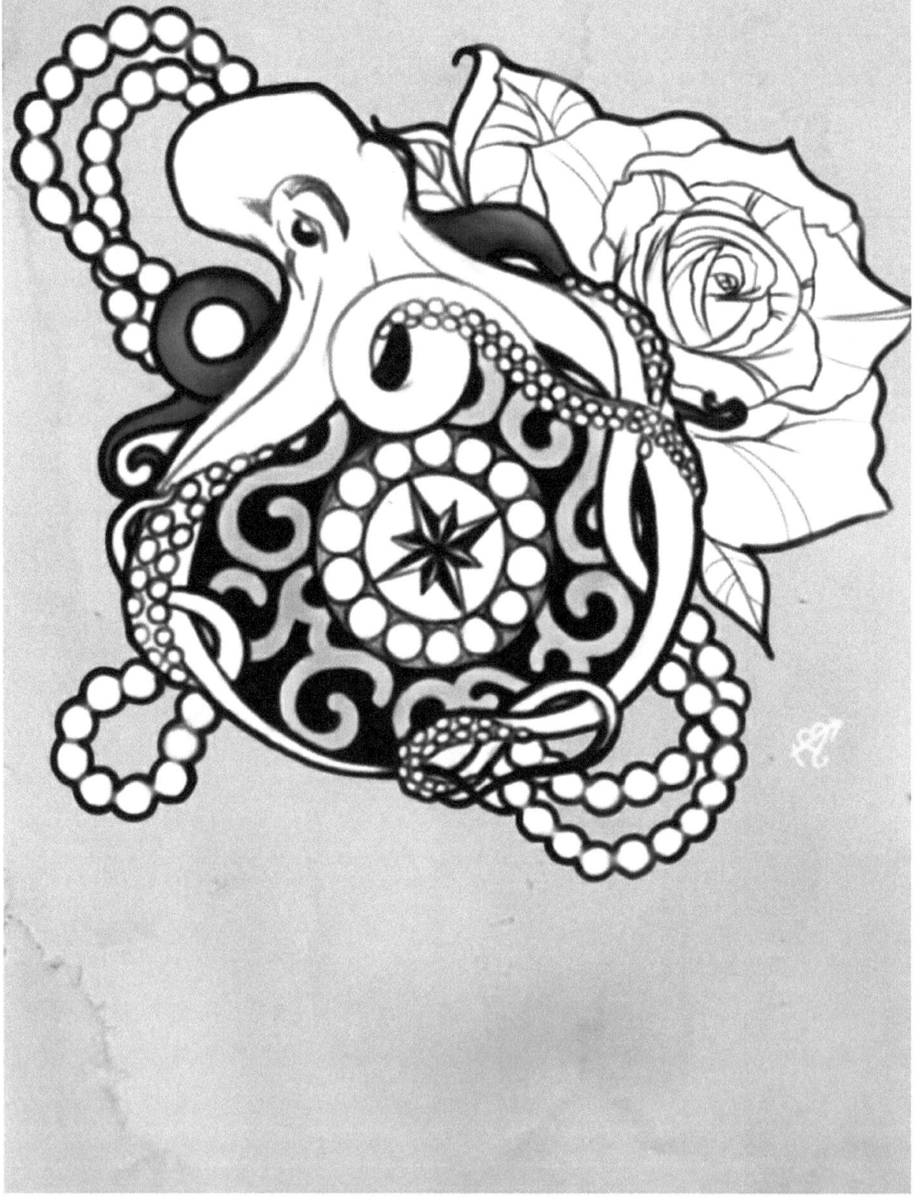

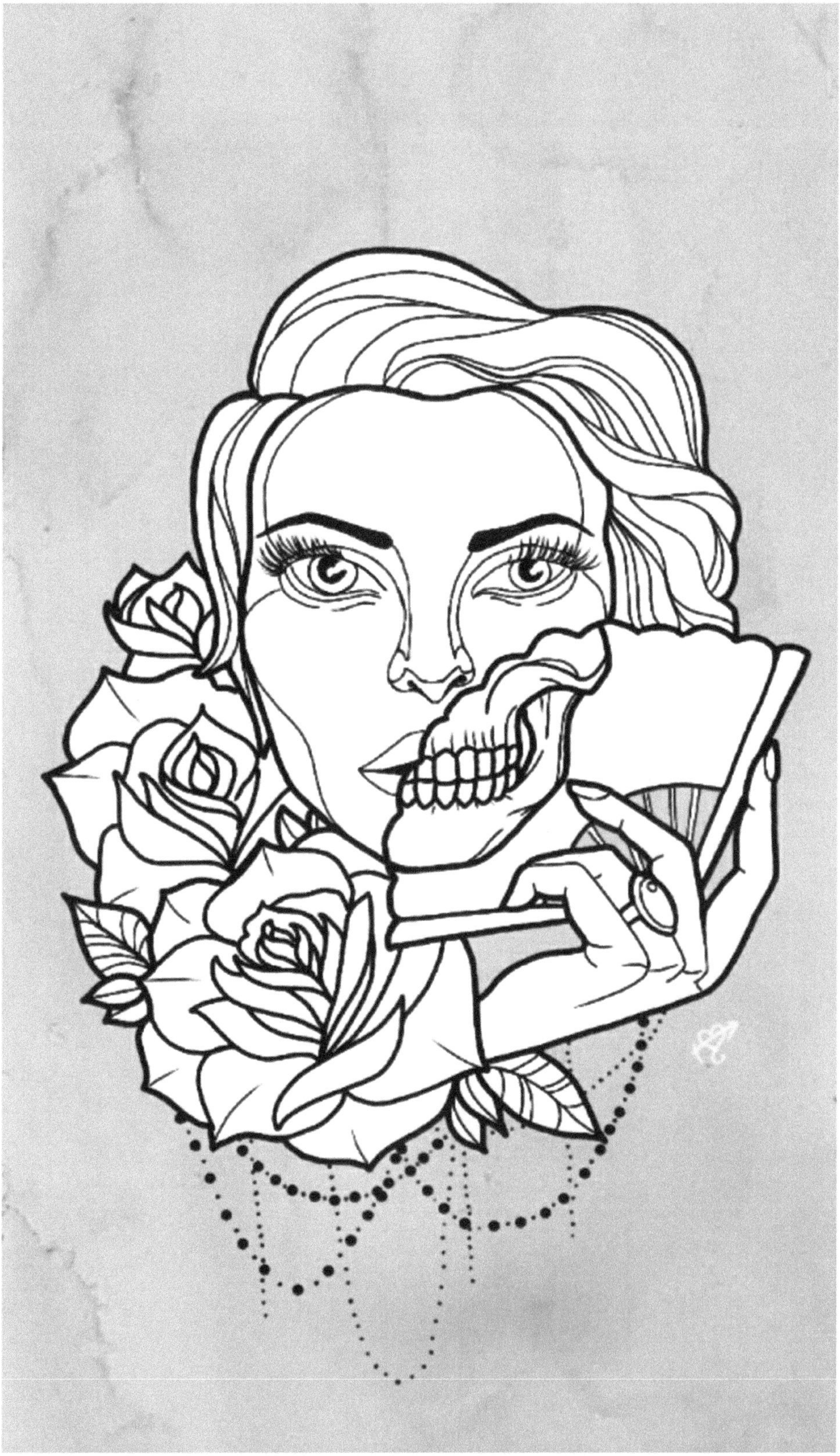

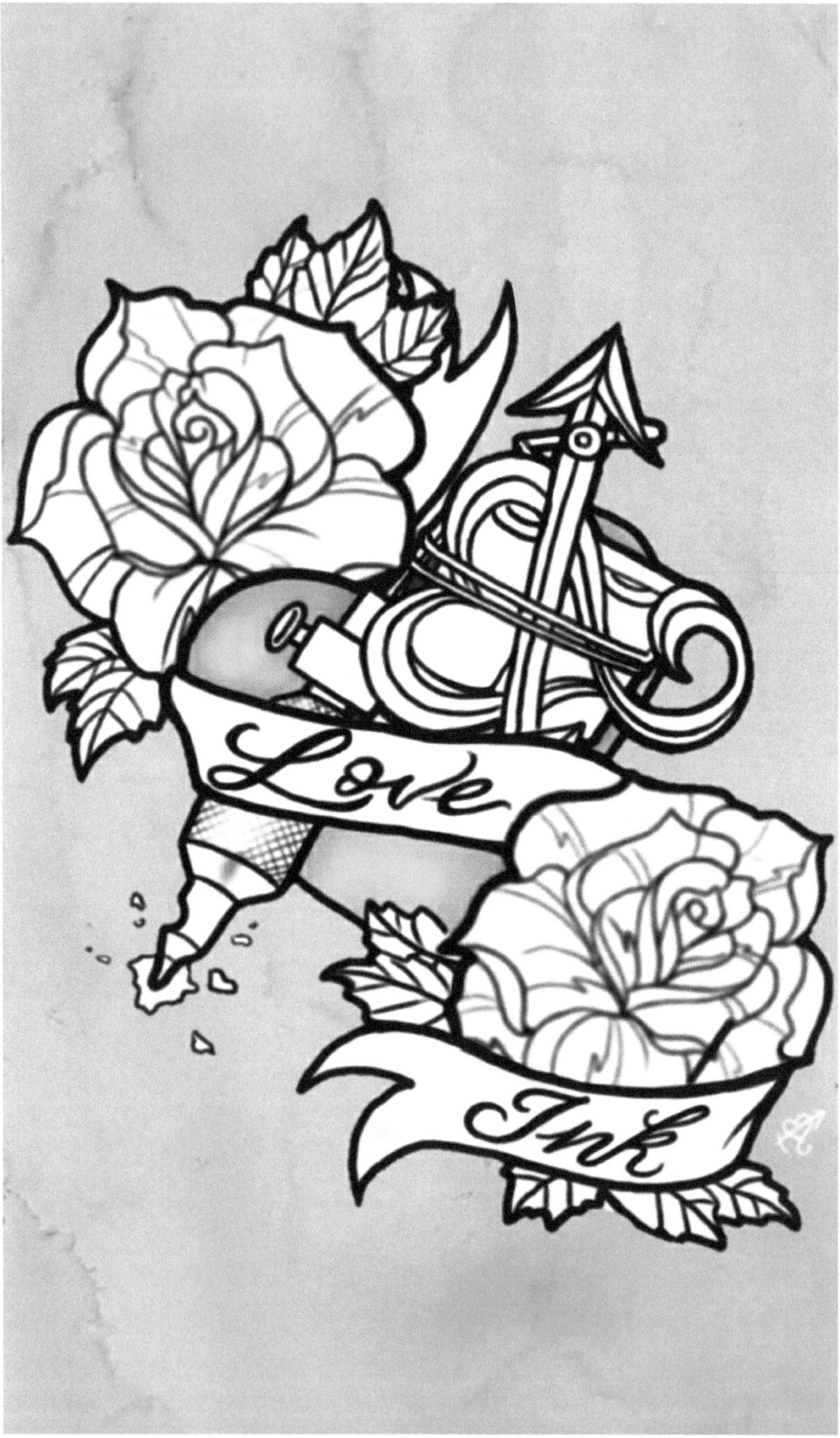
Love
Ink

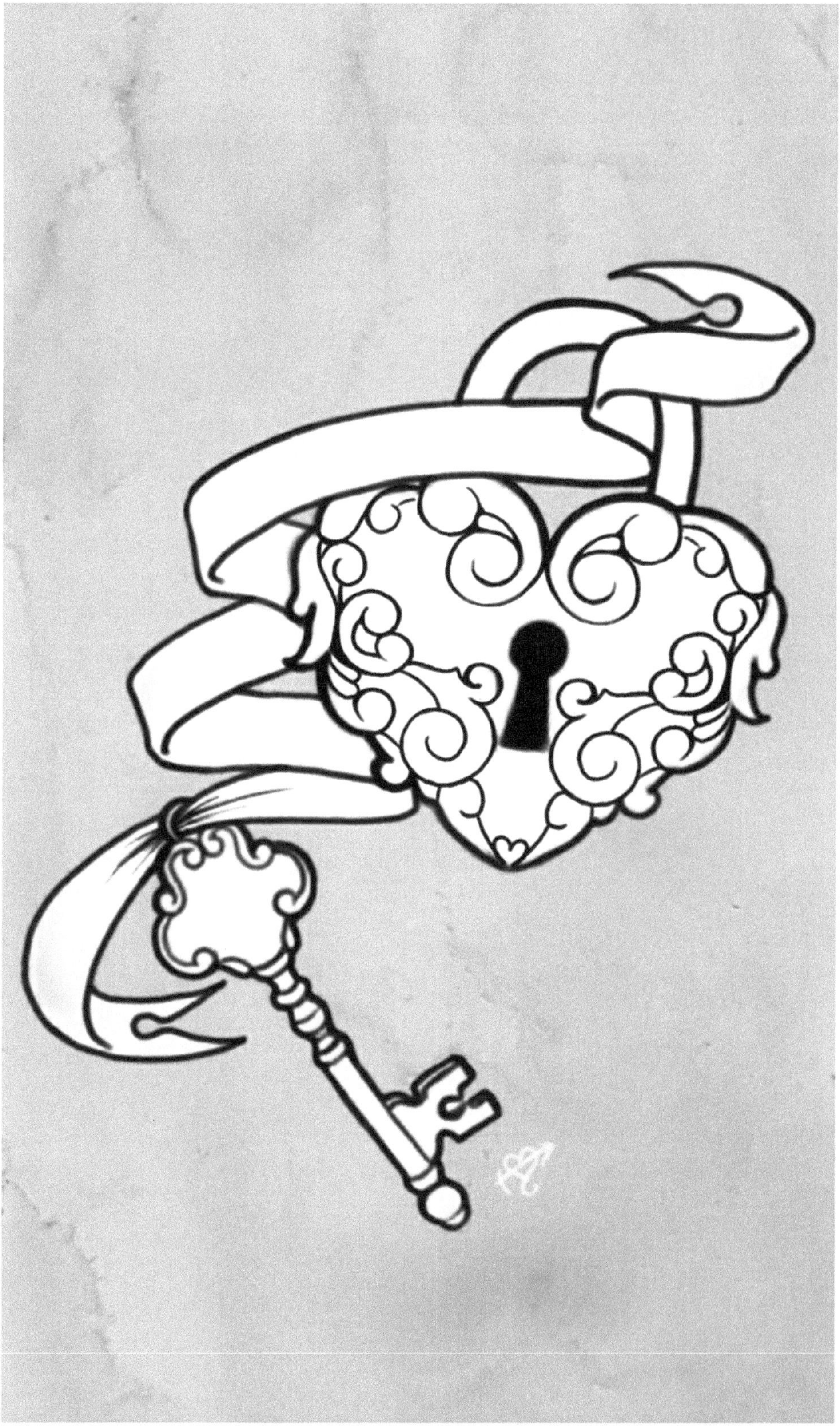

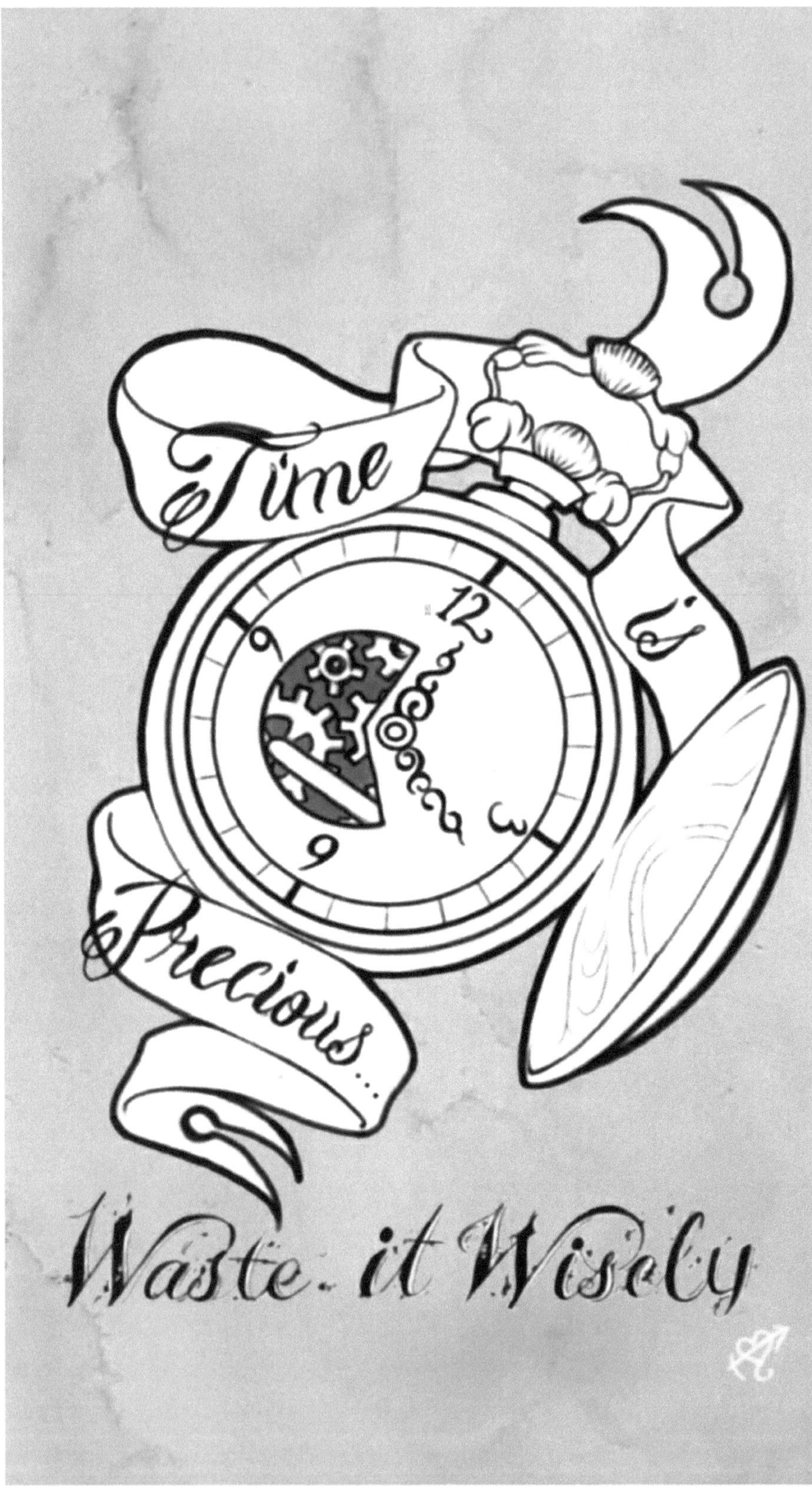
Time
is
Precious...
Waste it Wisely

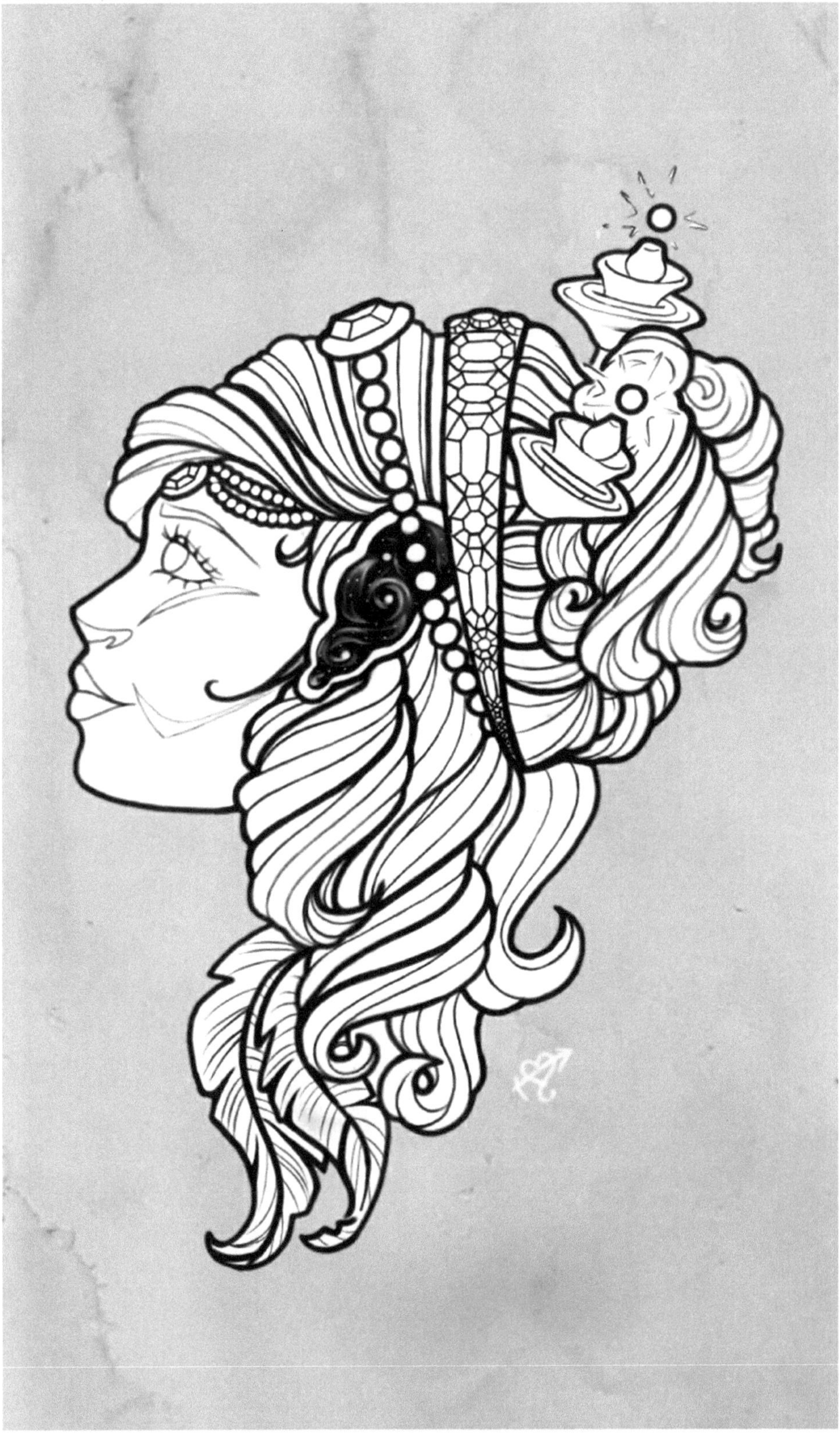

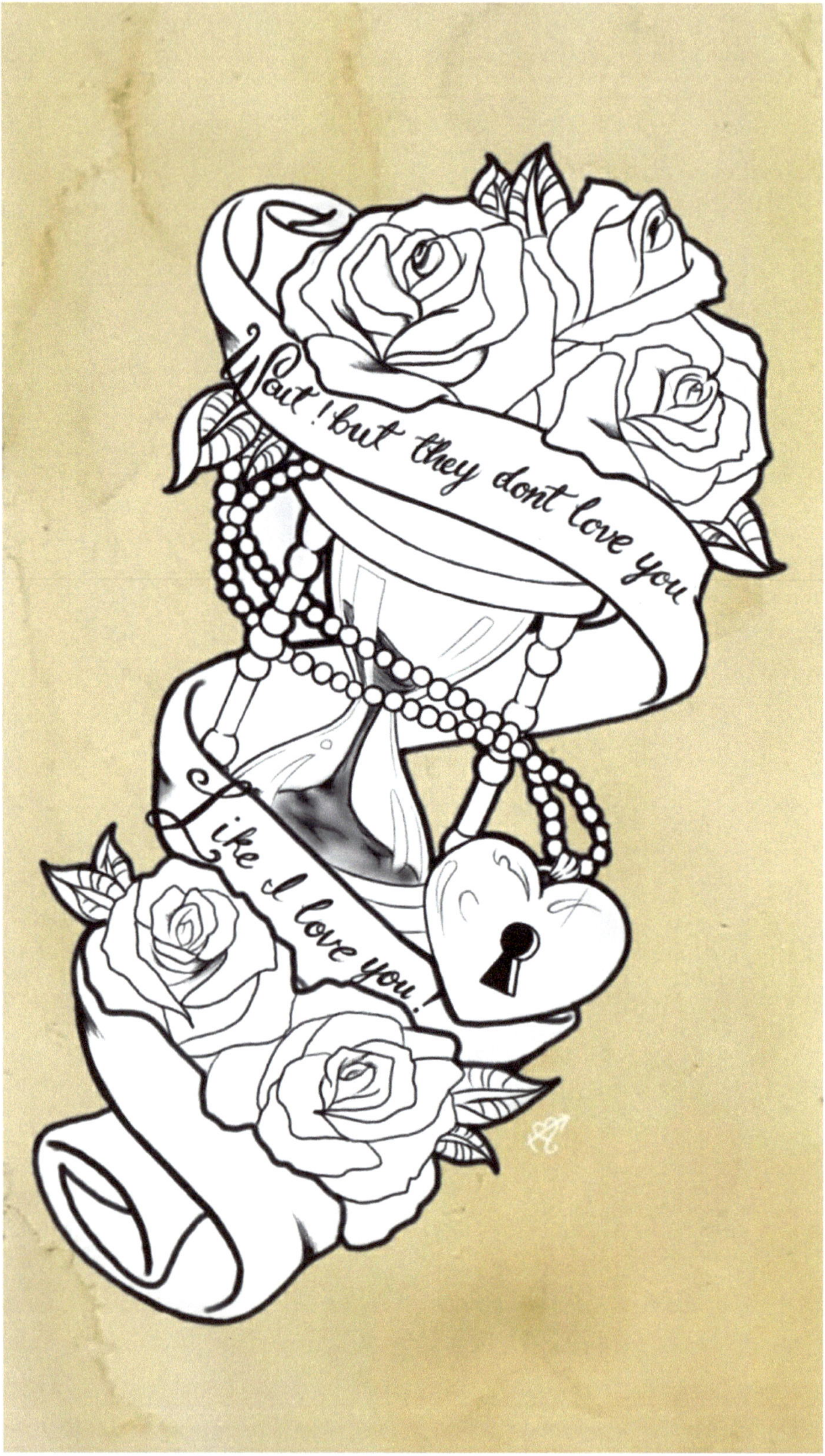
Wait! but they dont love you
Like I love you!

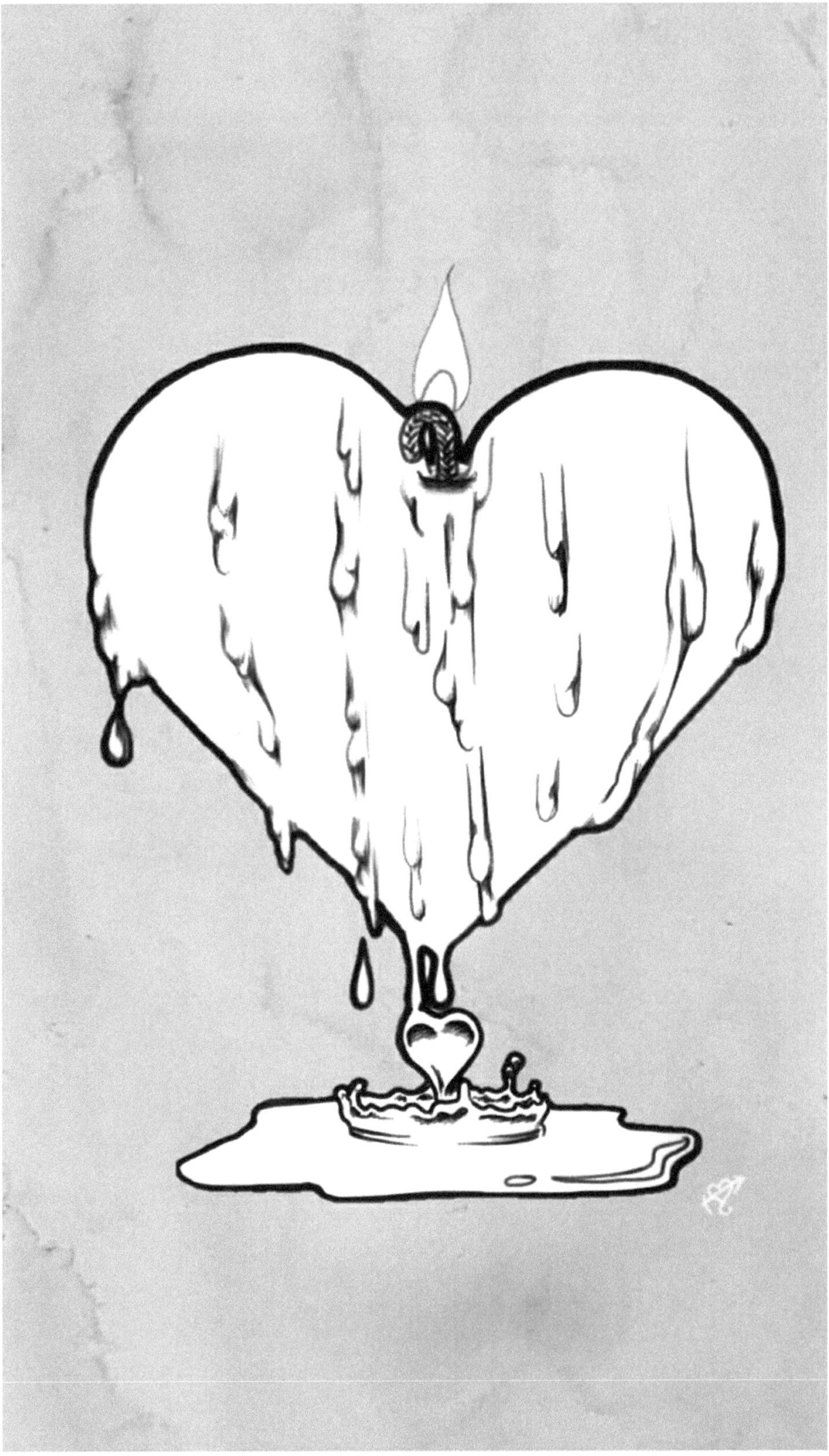

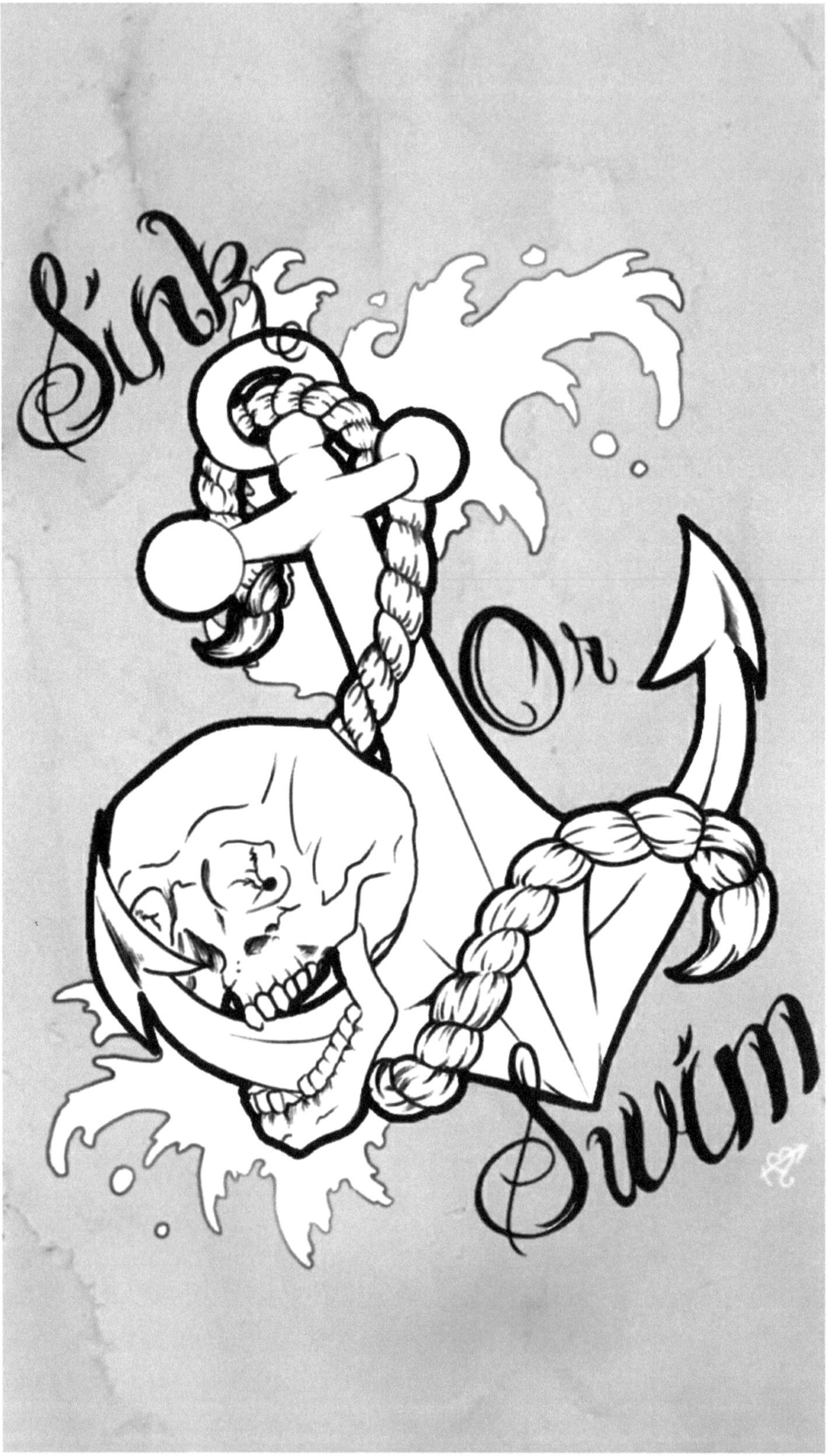
Sink
Or
Swim

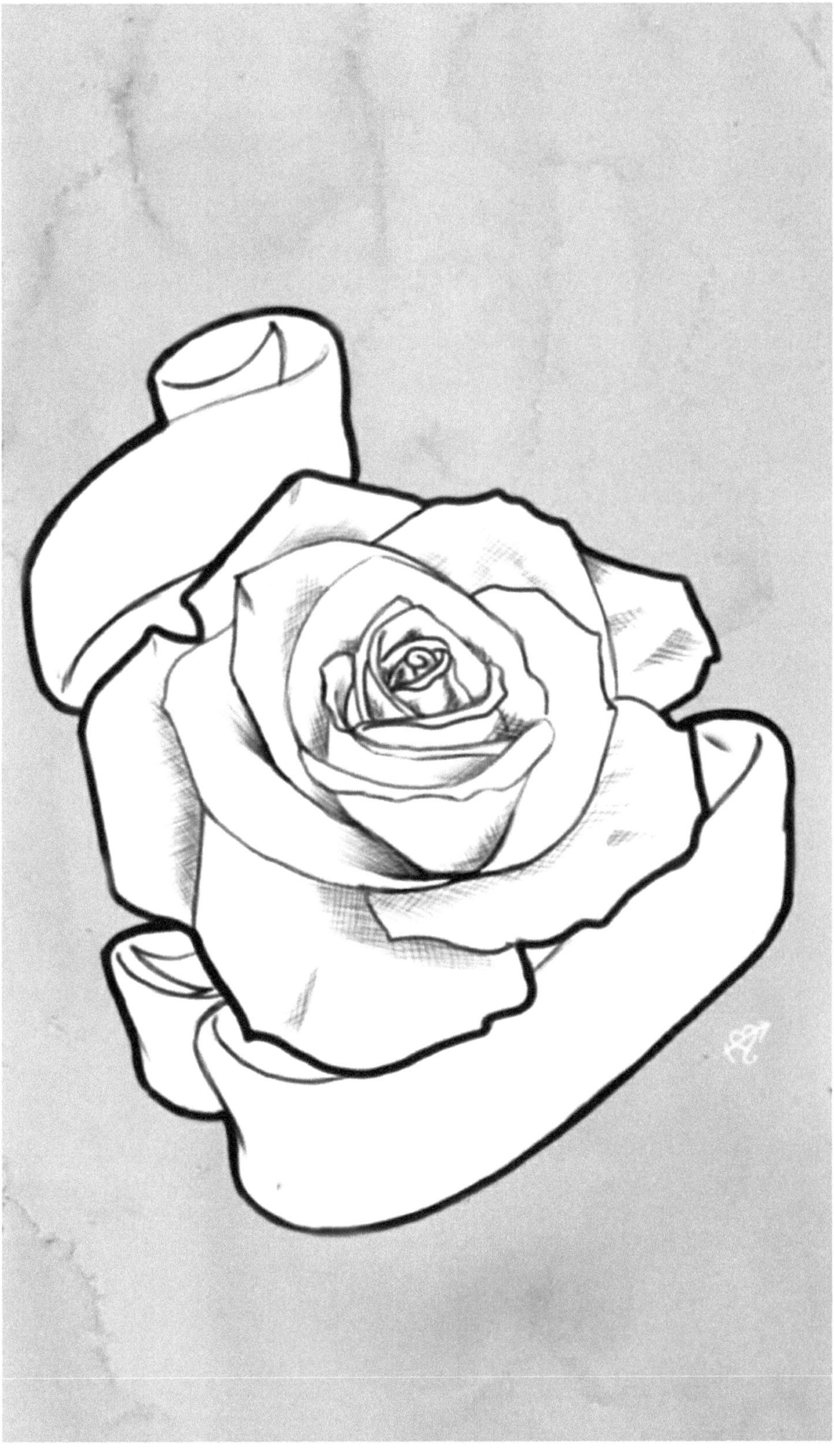

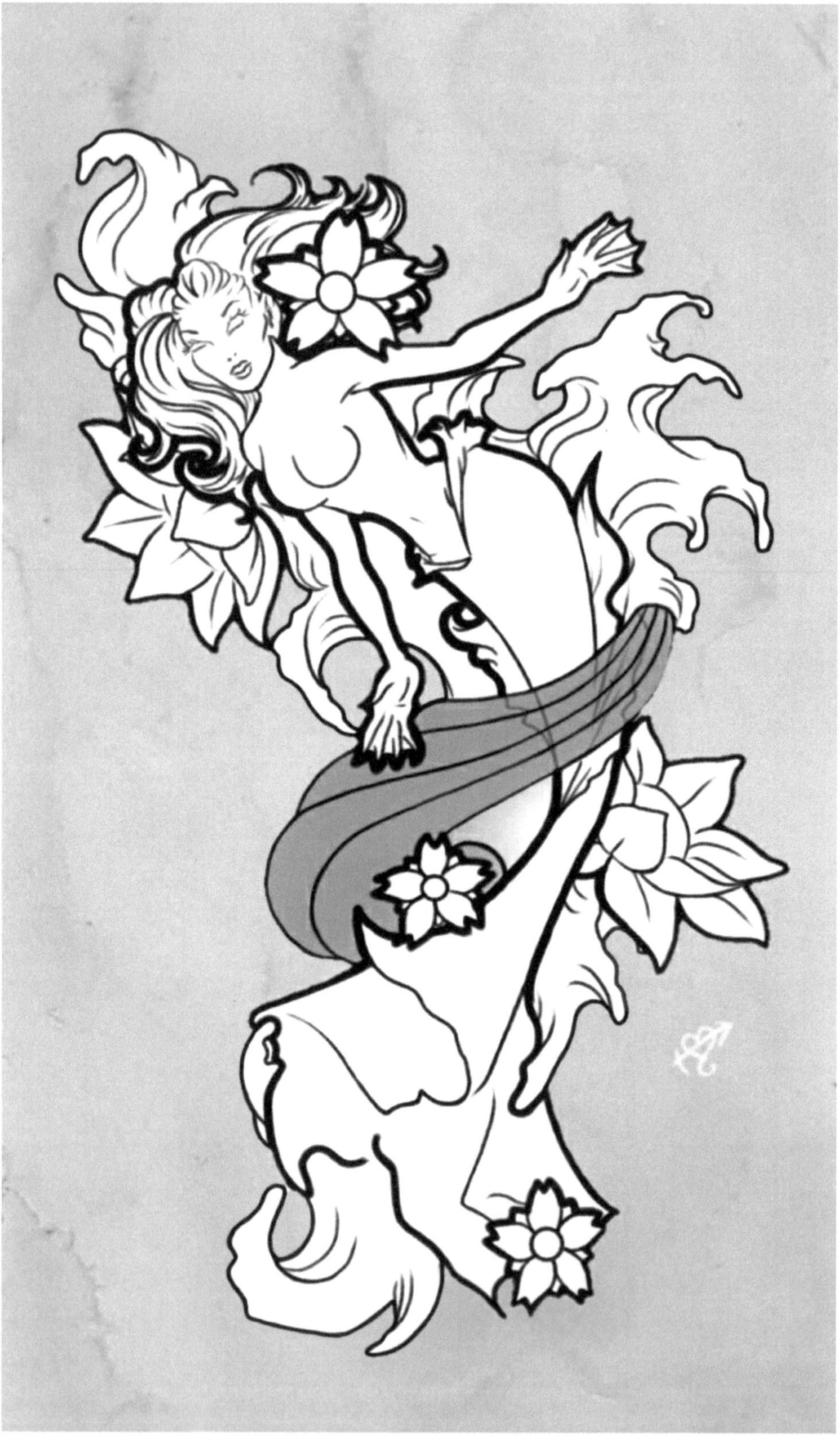

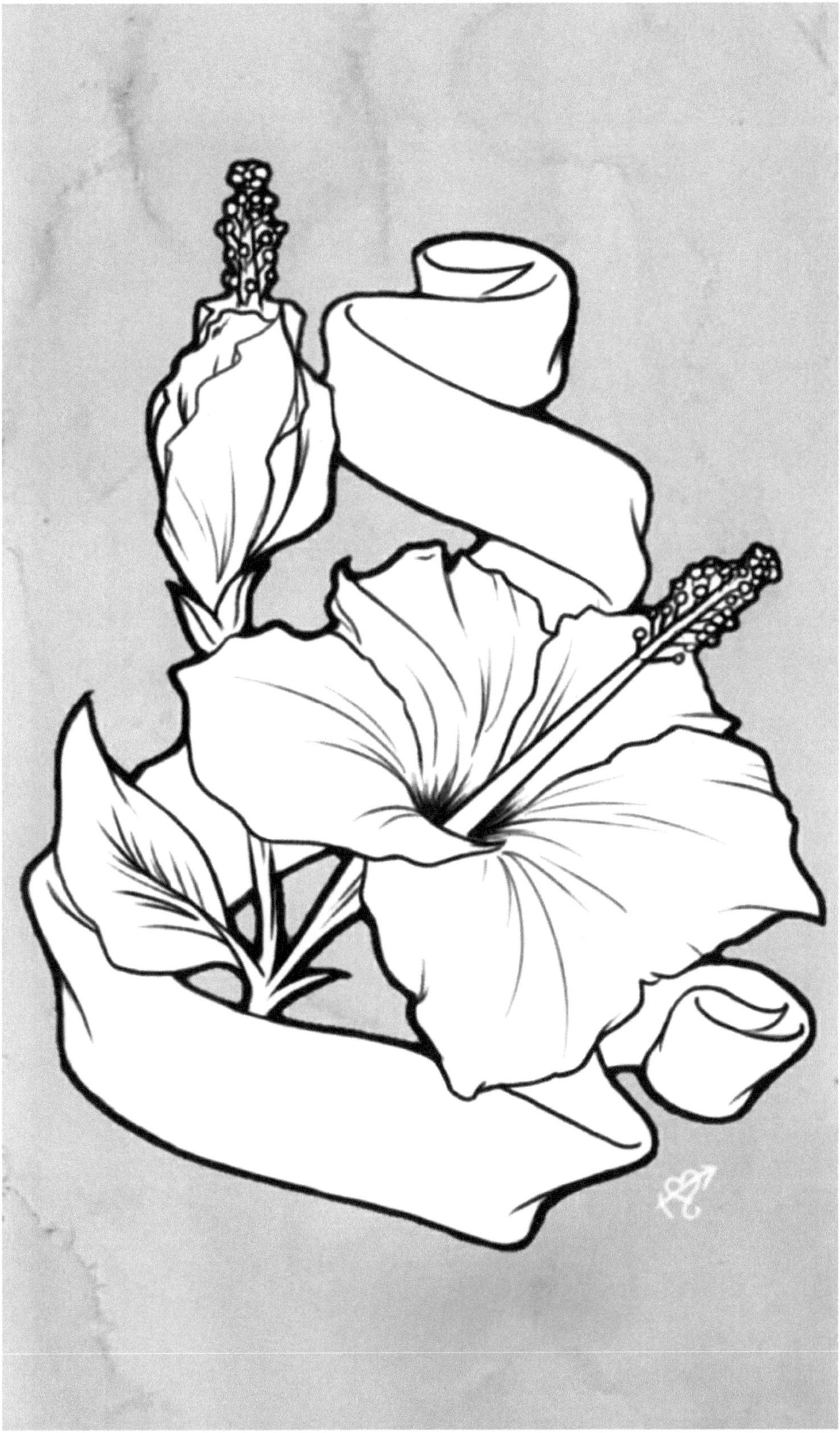

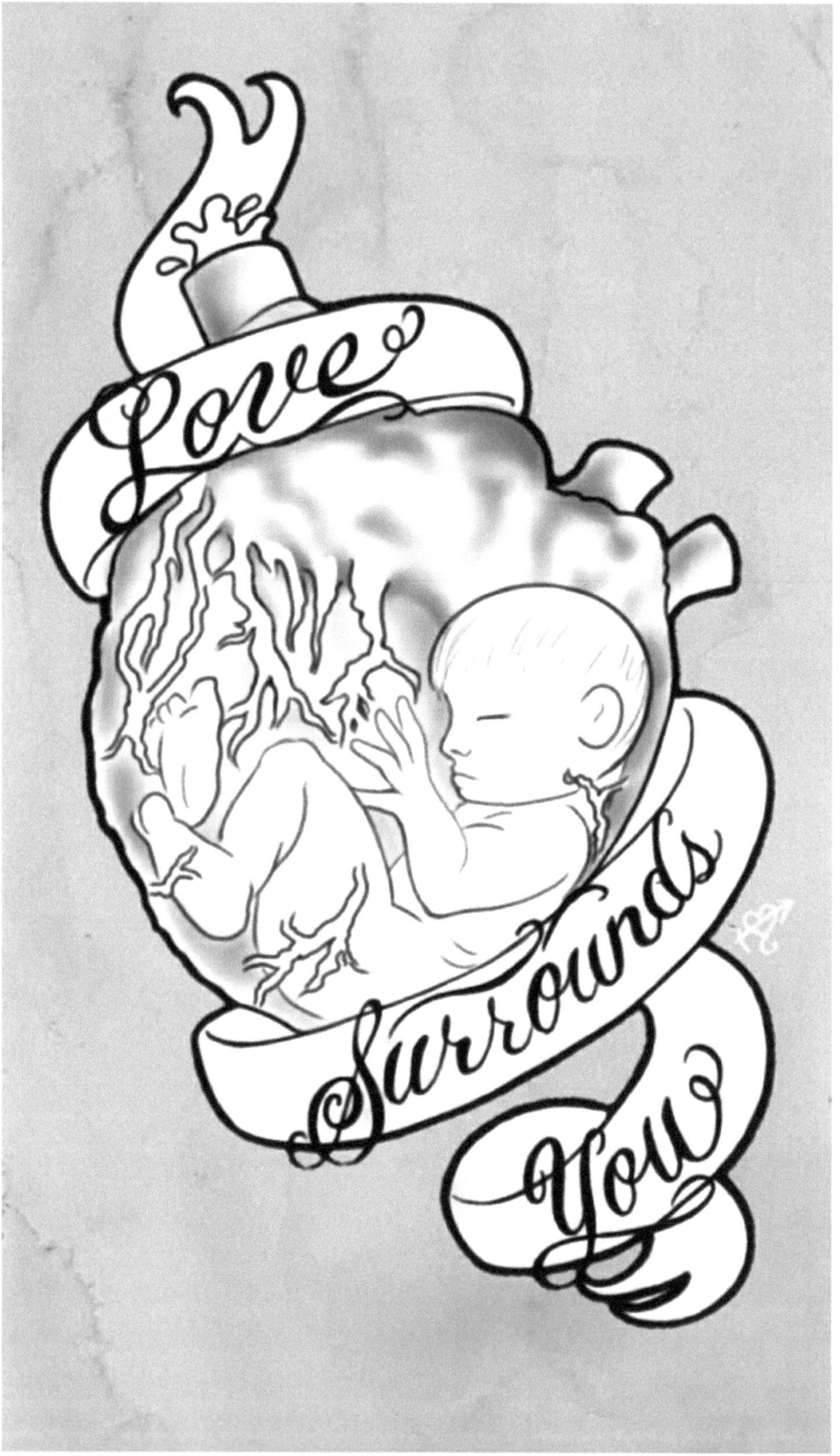
Love
Surrounds
You

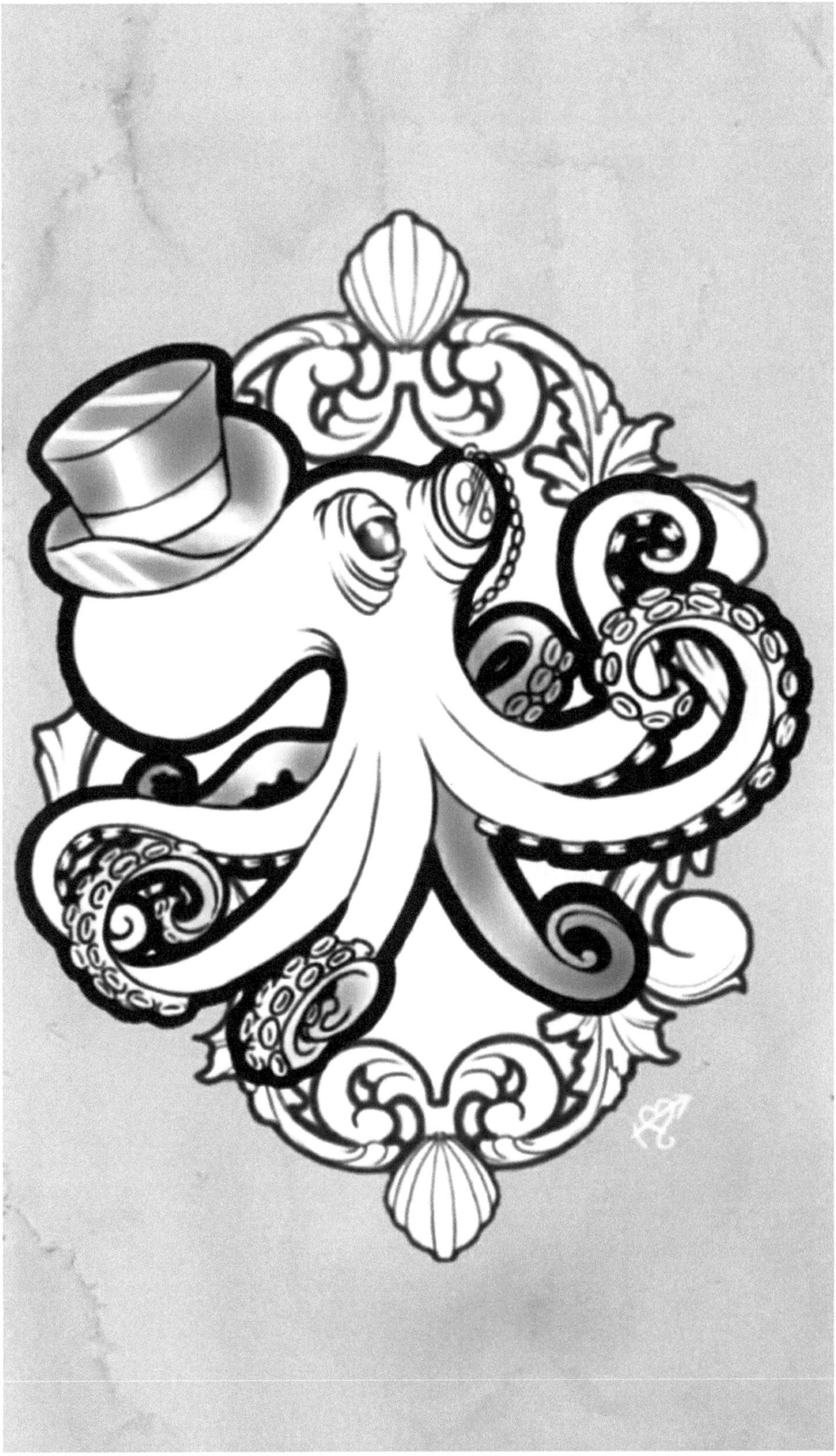

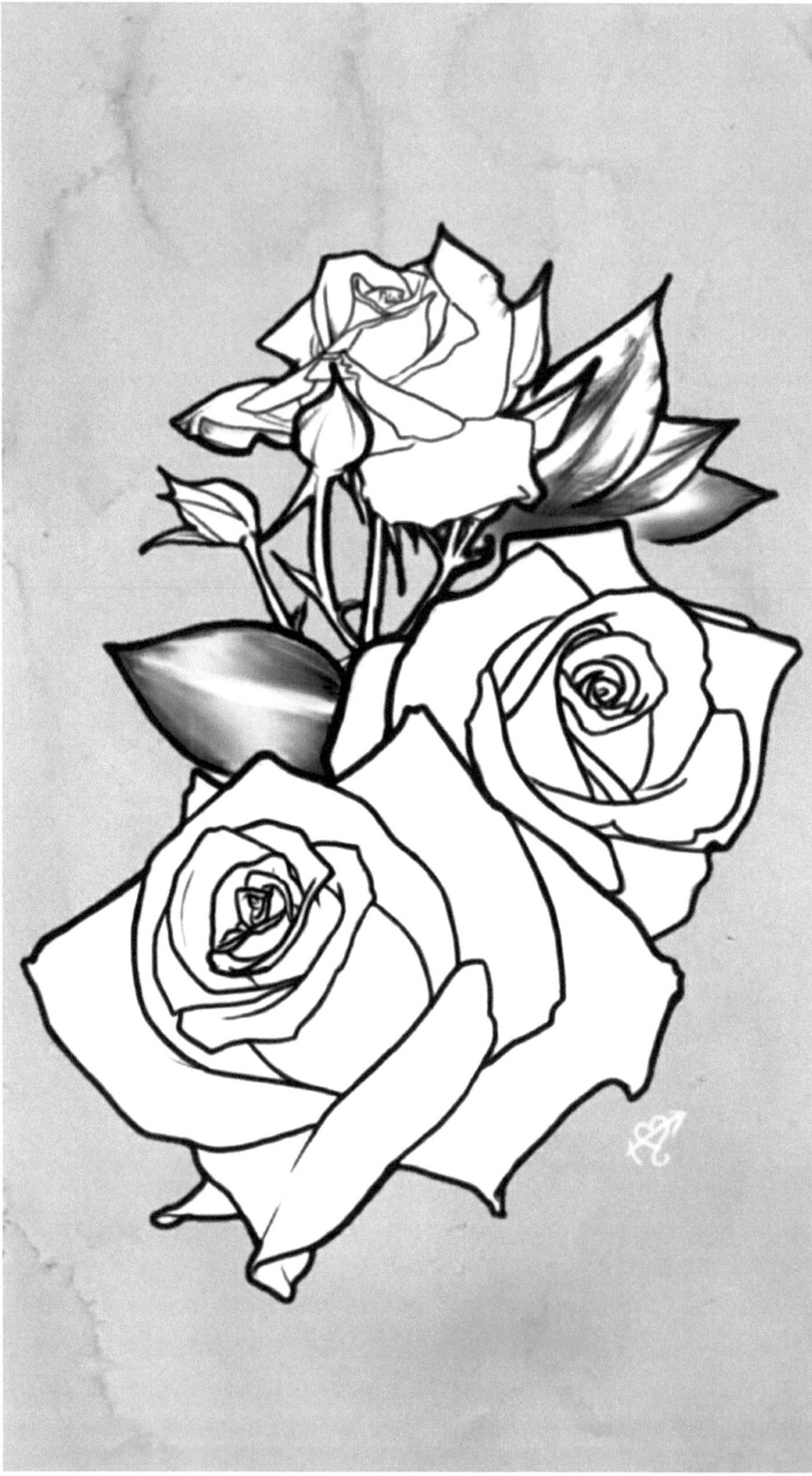

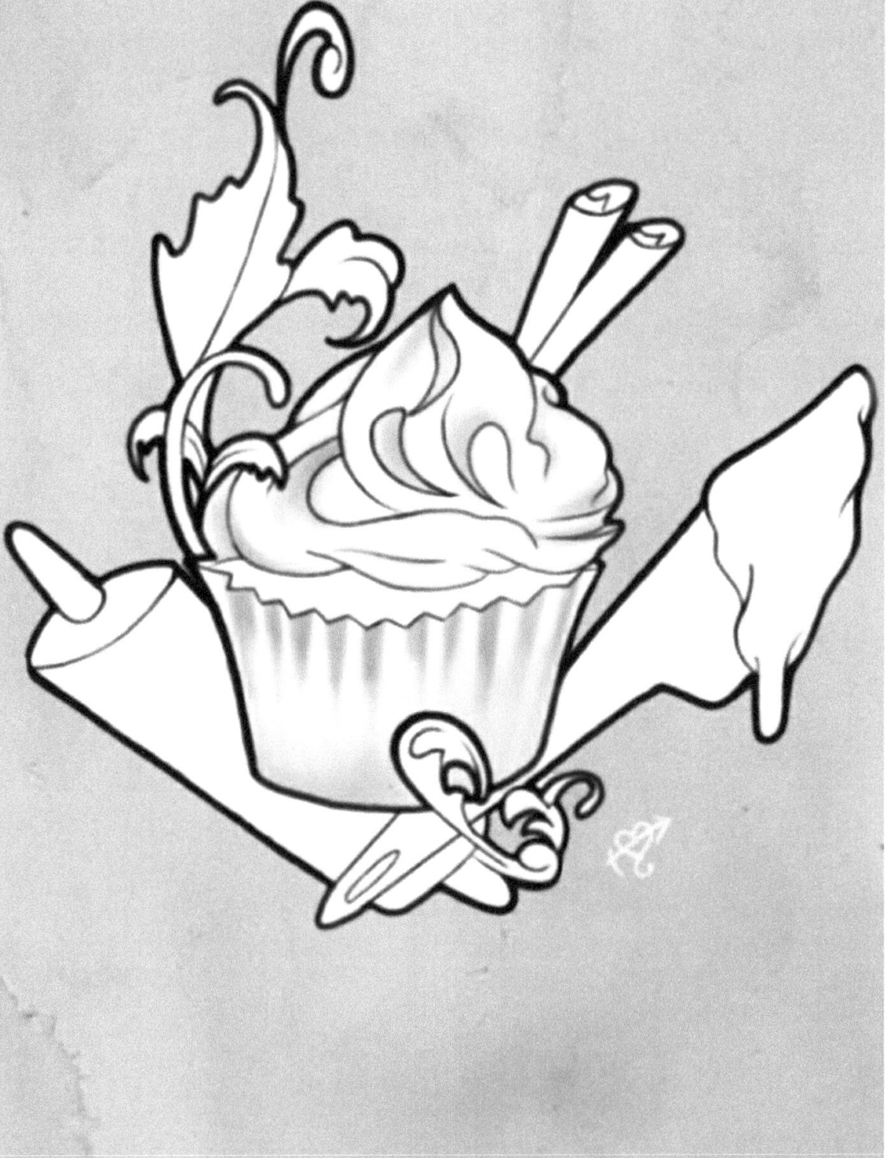

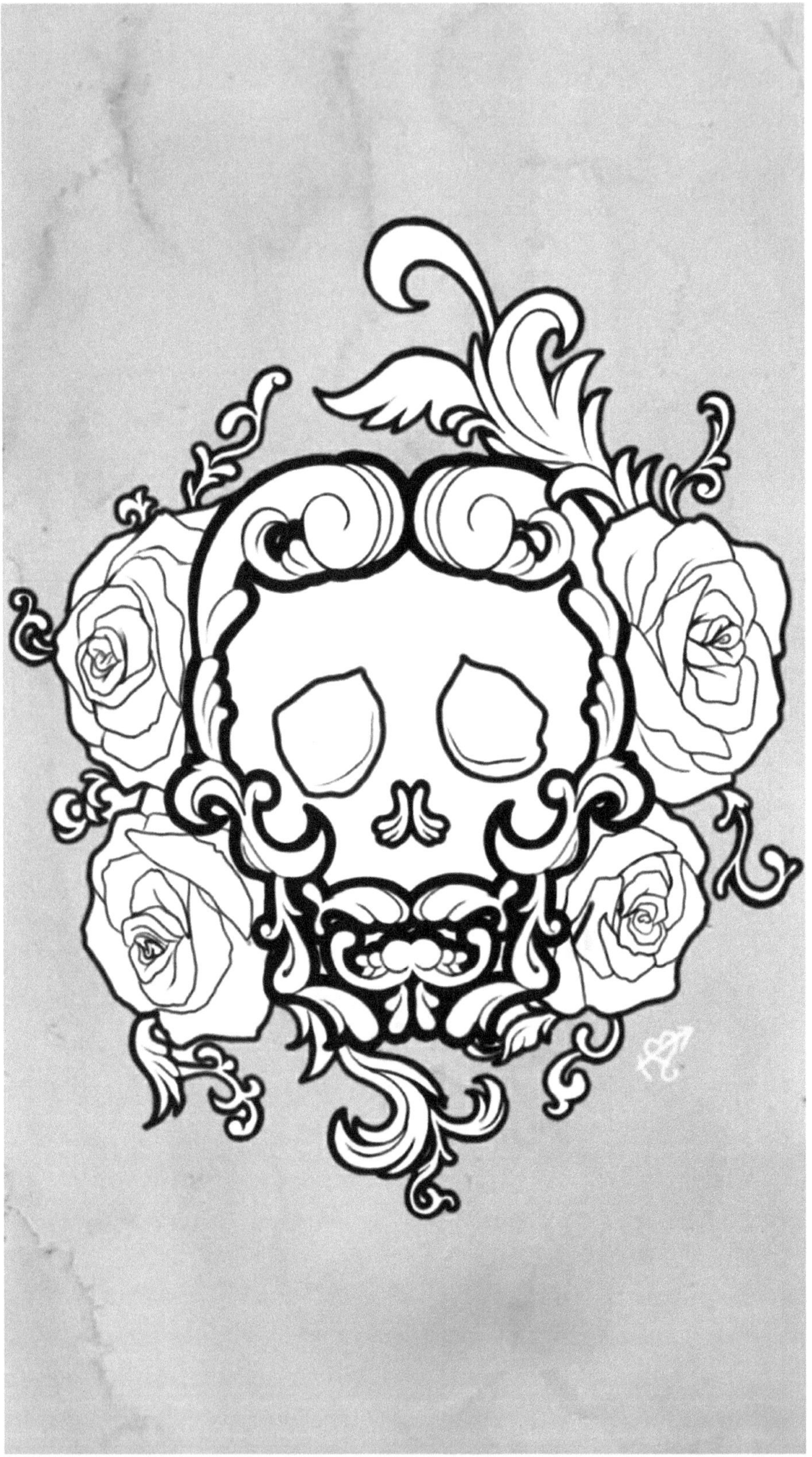

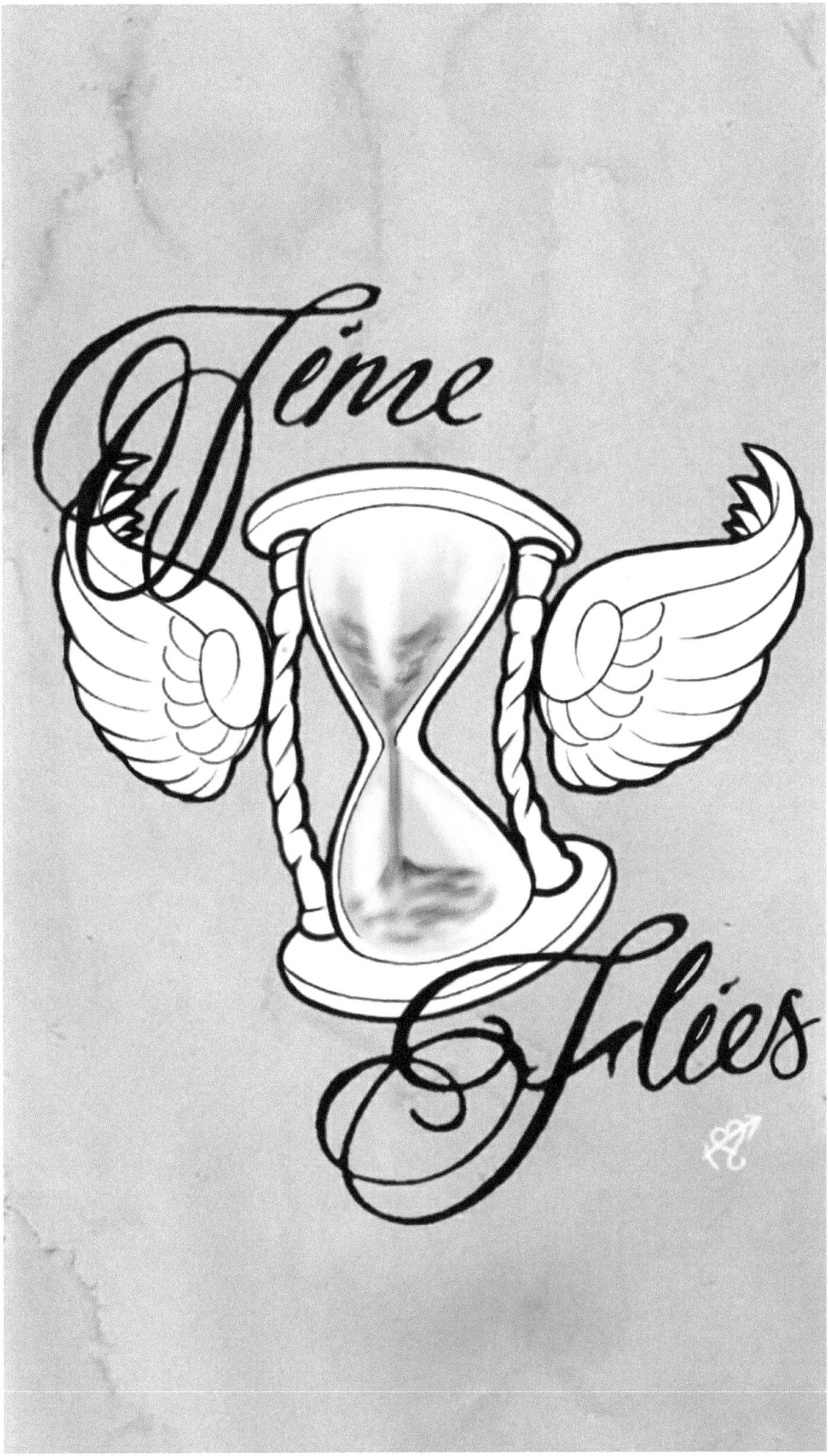
Time
Flies

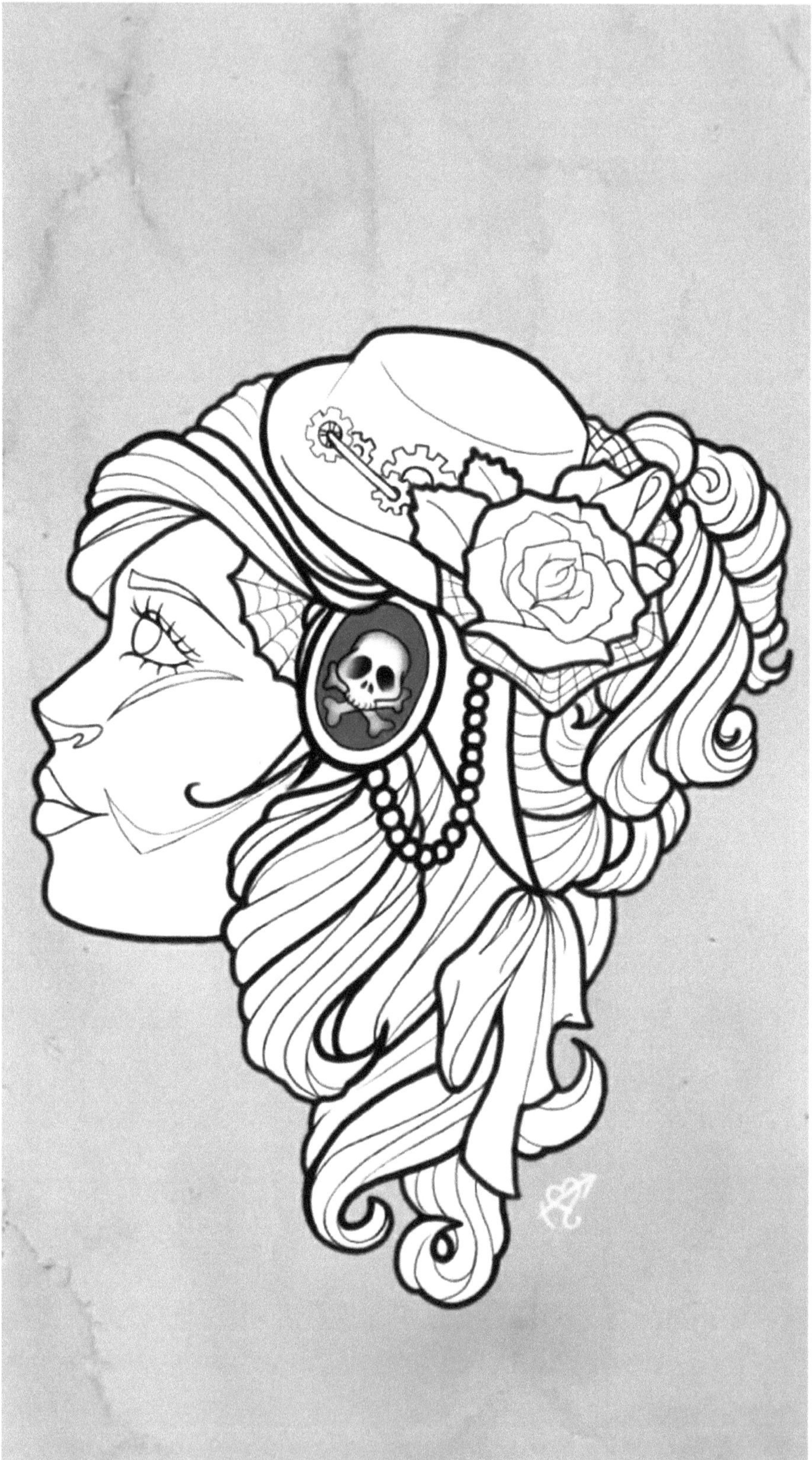

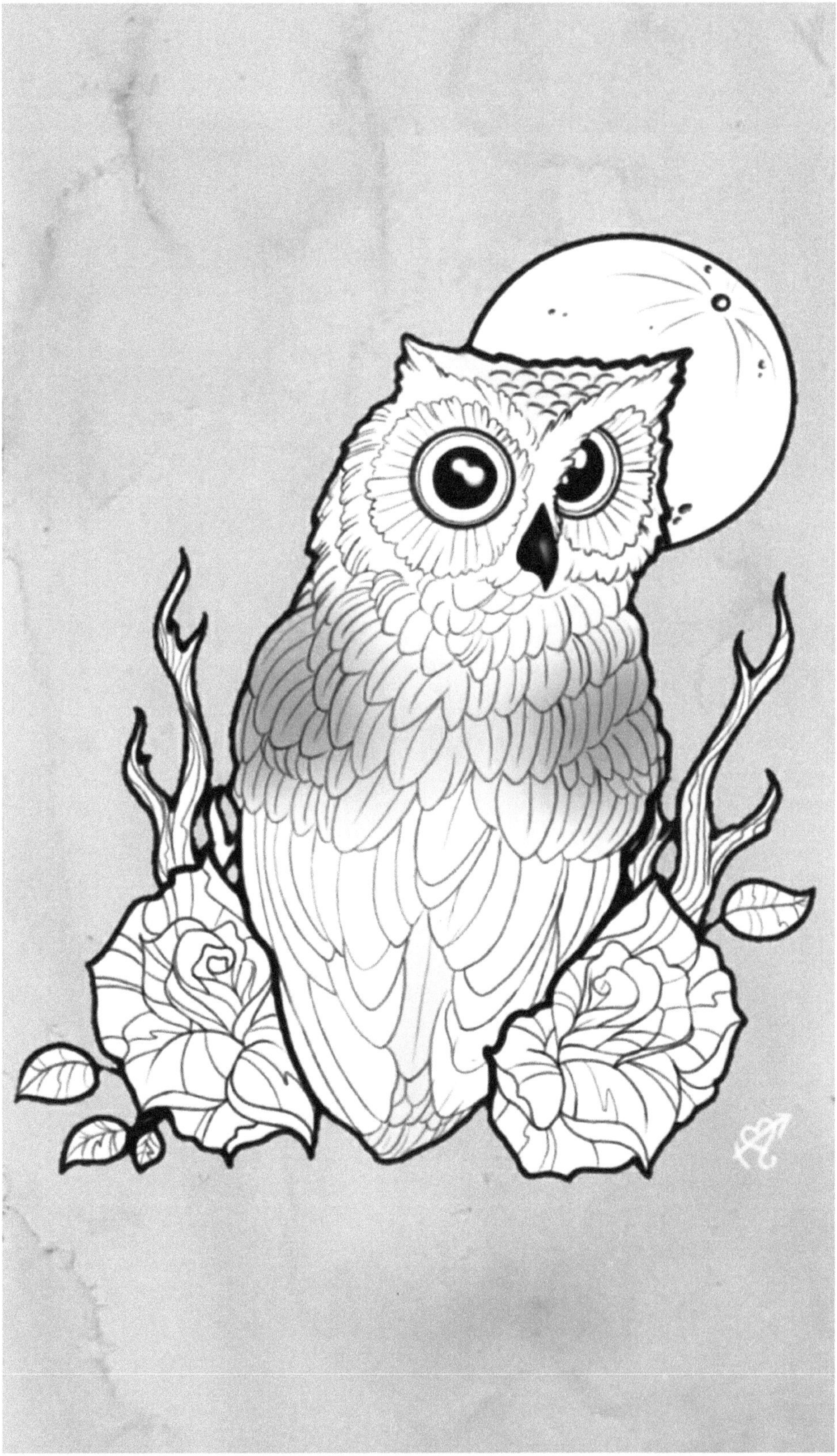

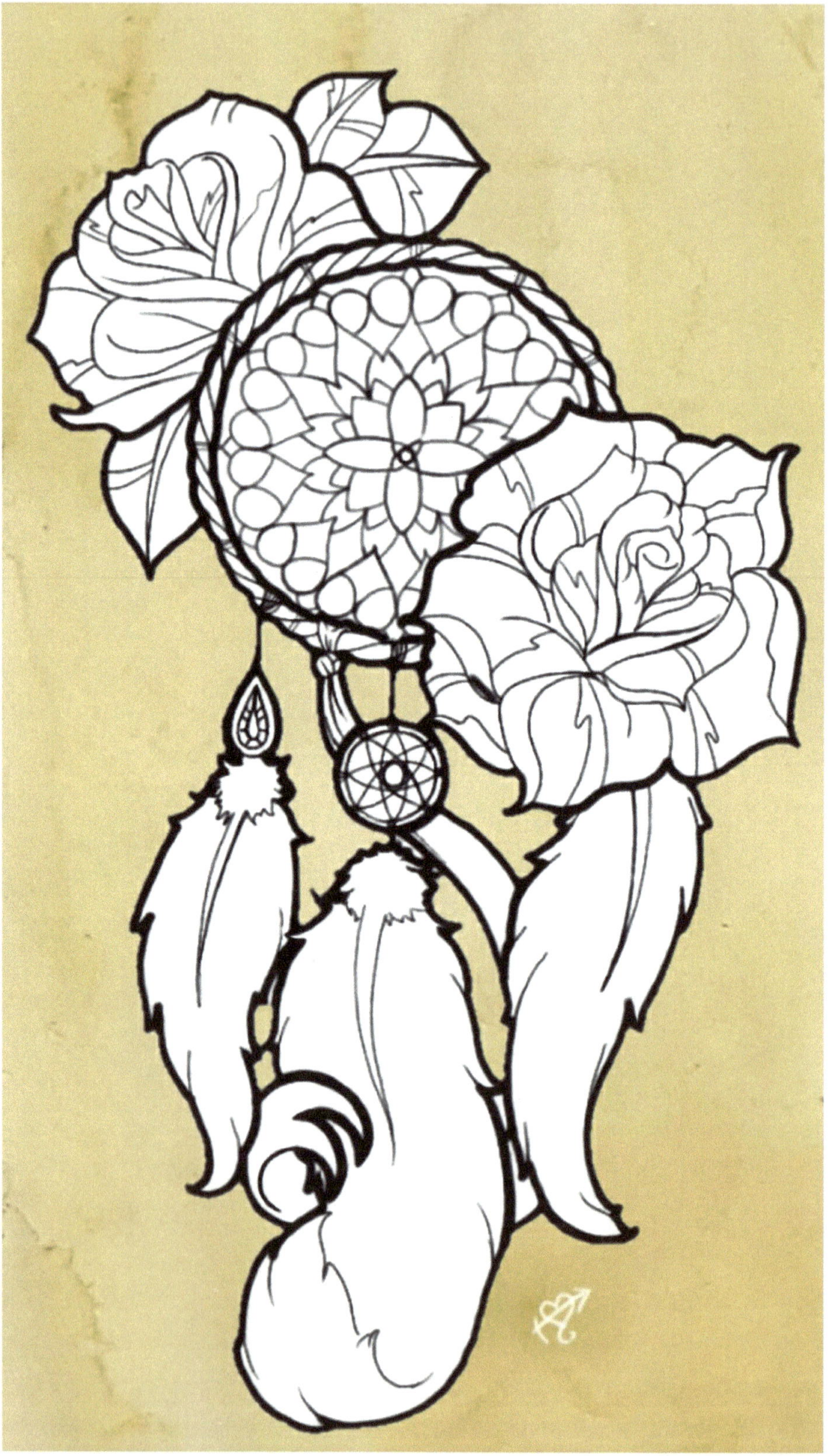

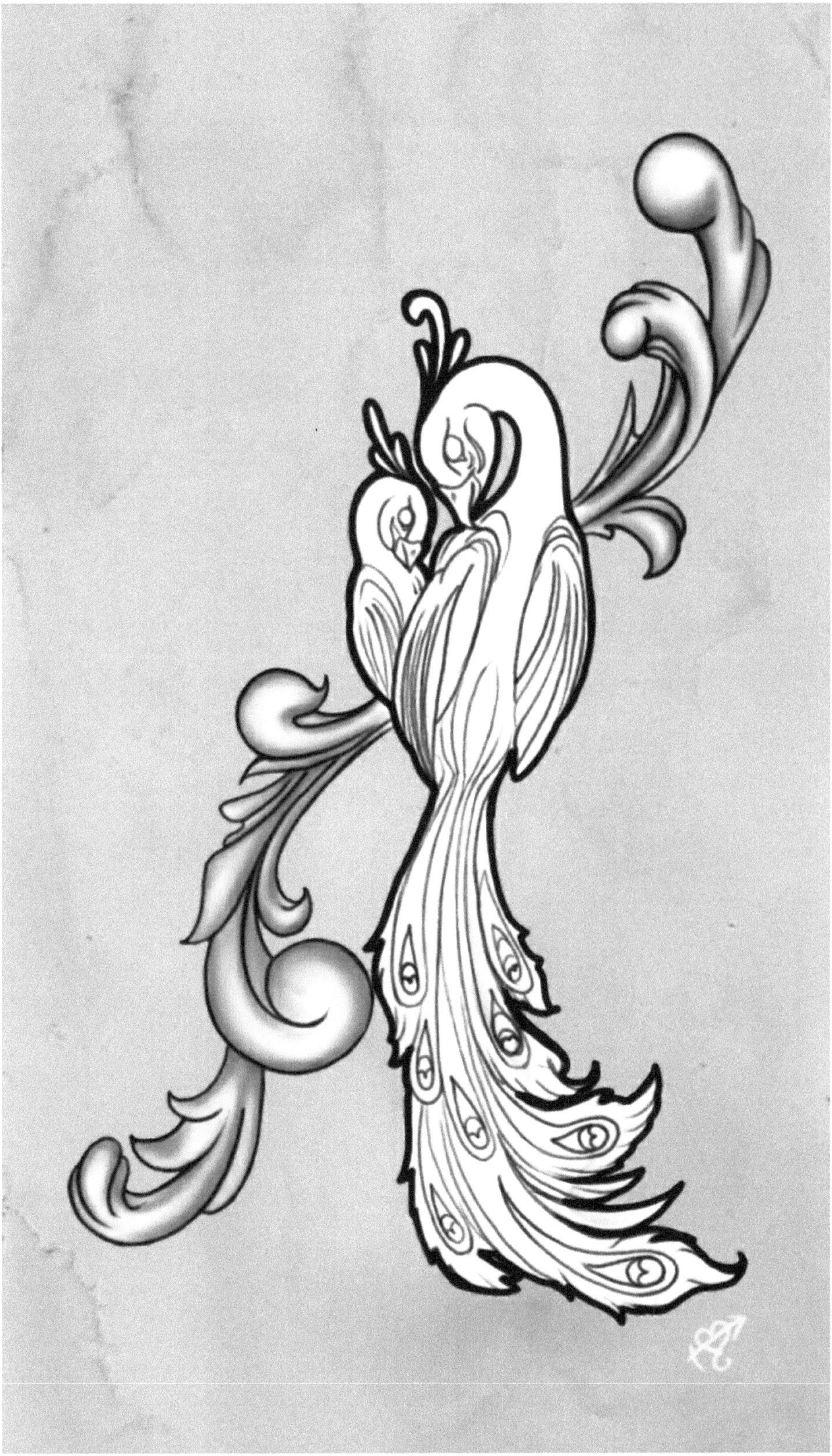

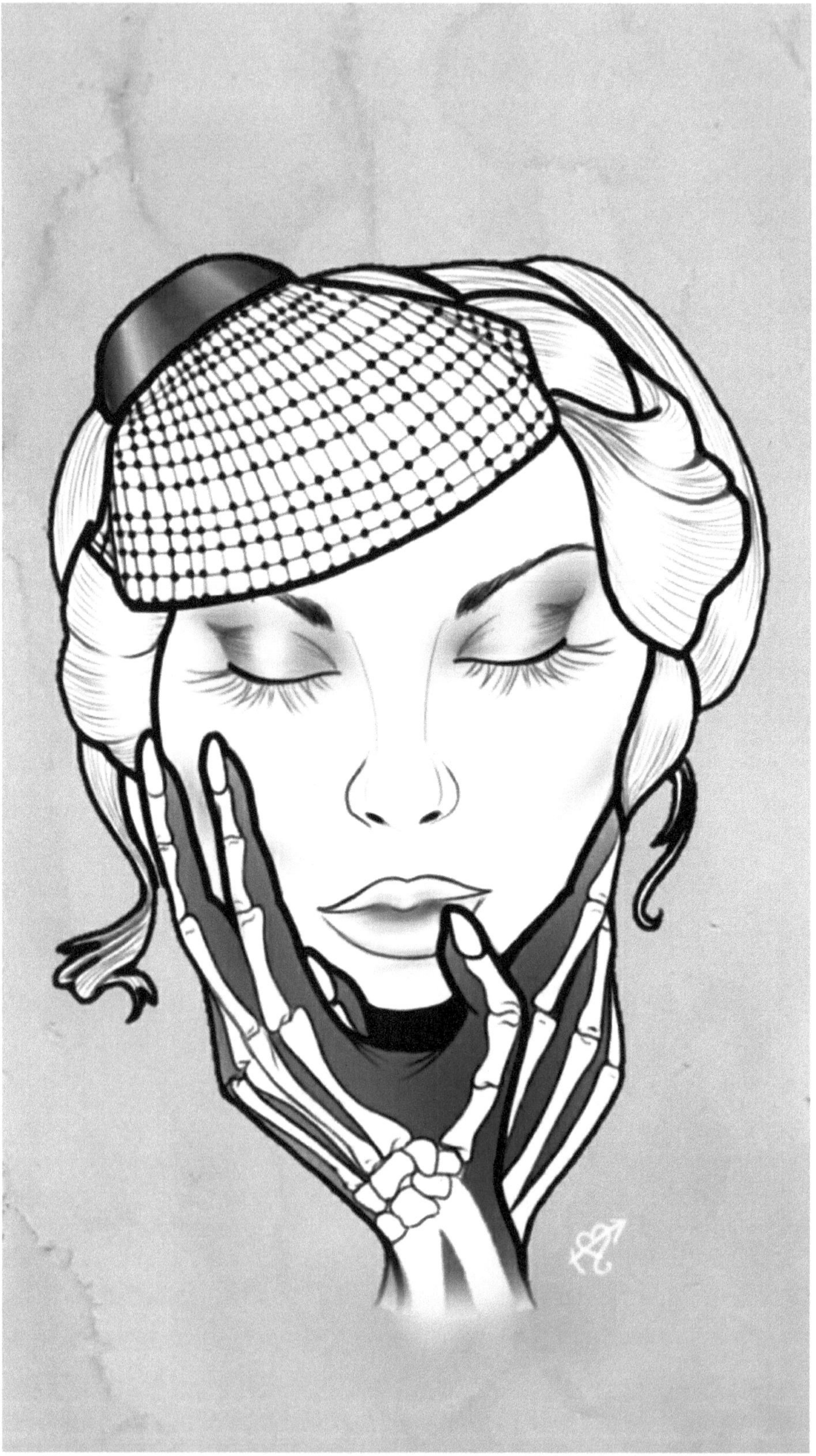

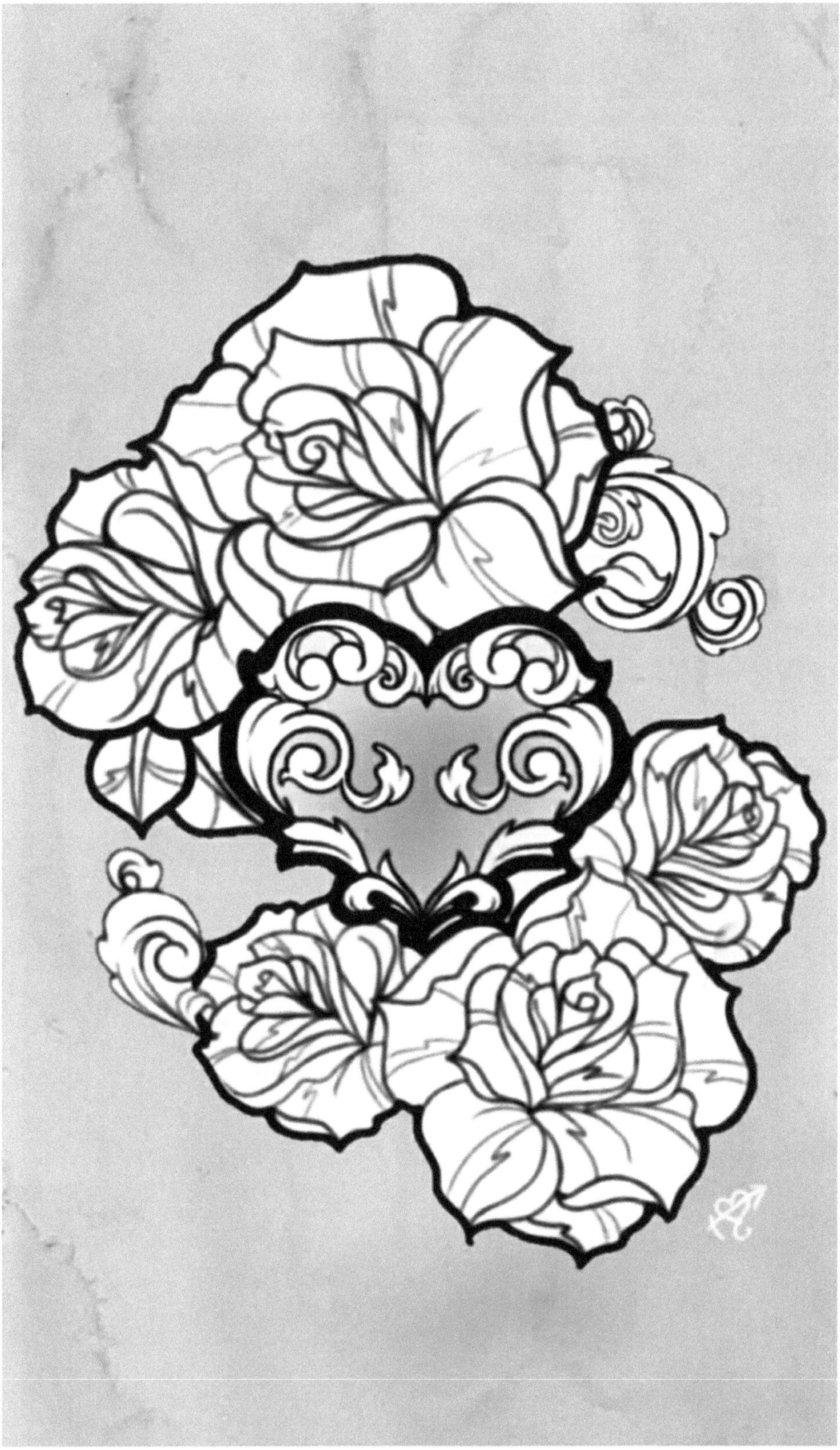

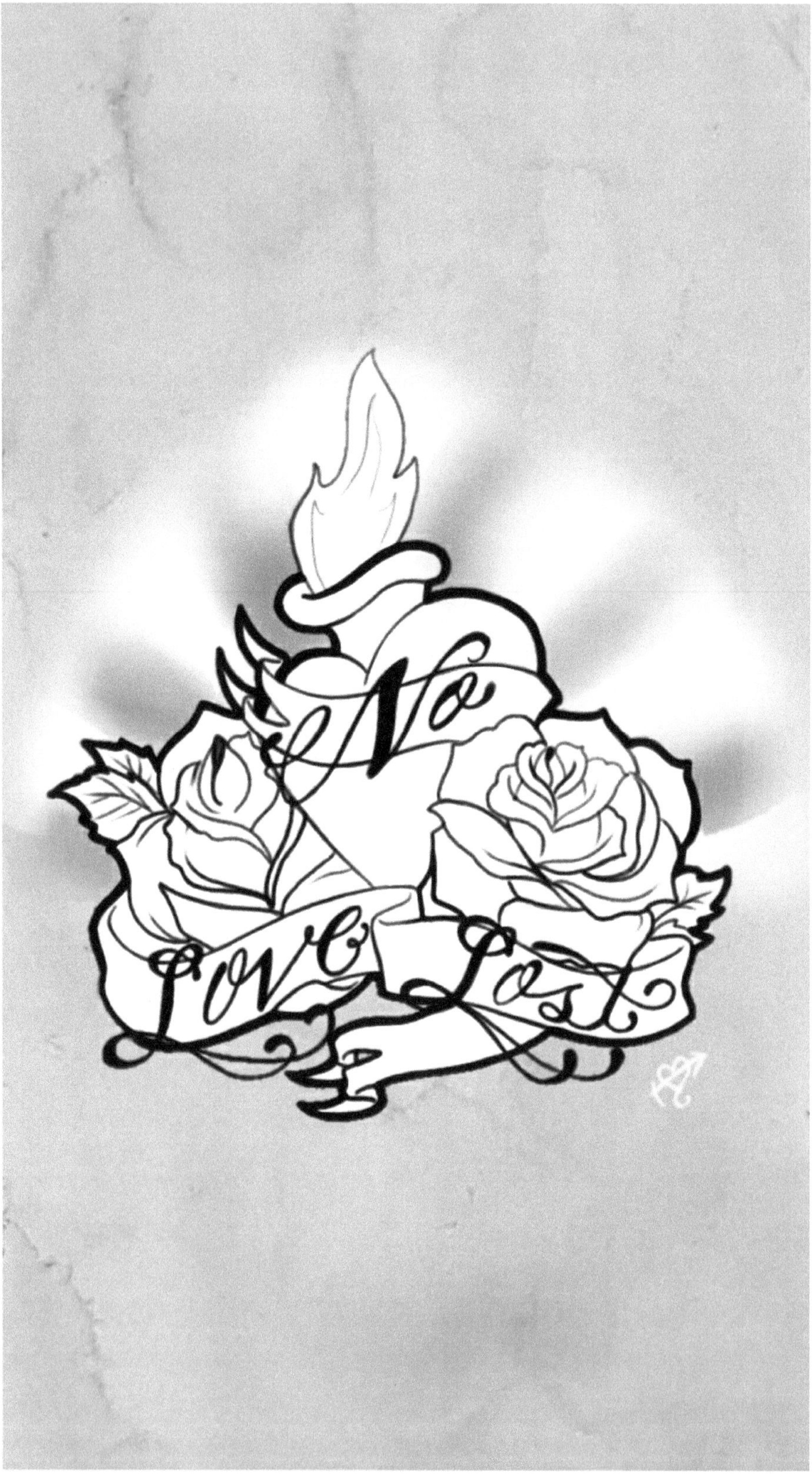
No
Love Lost

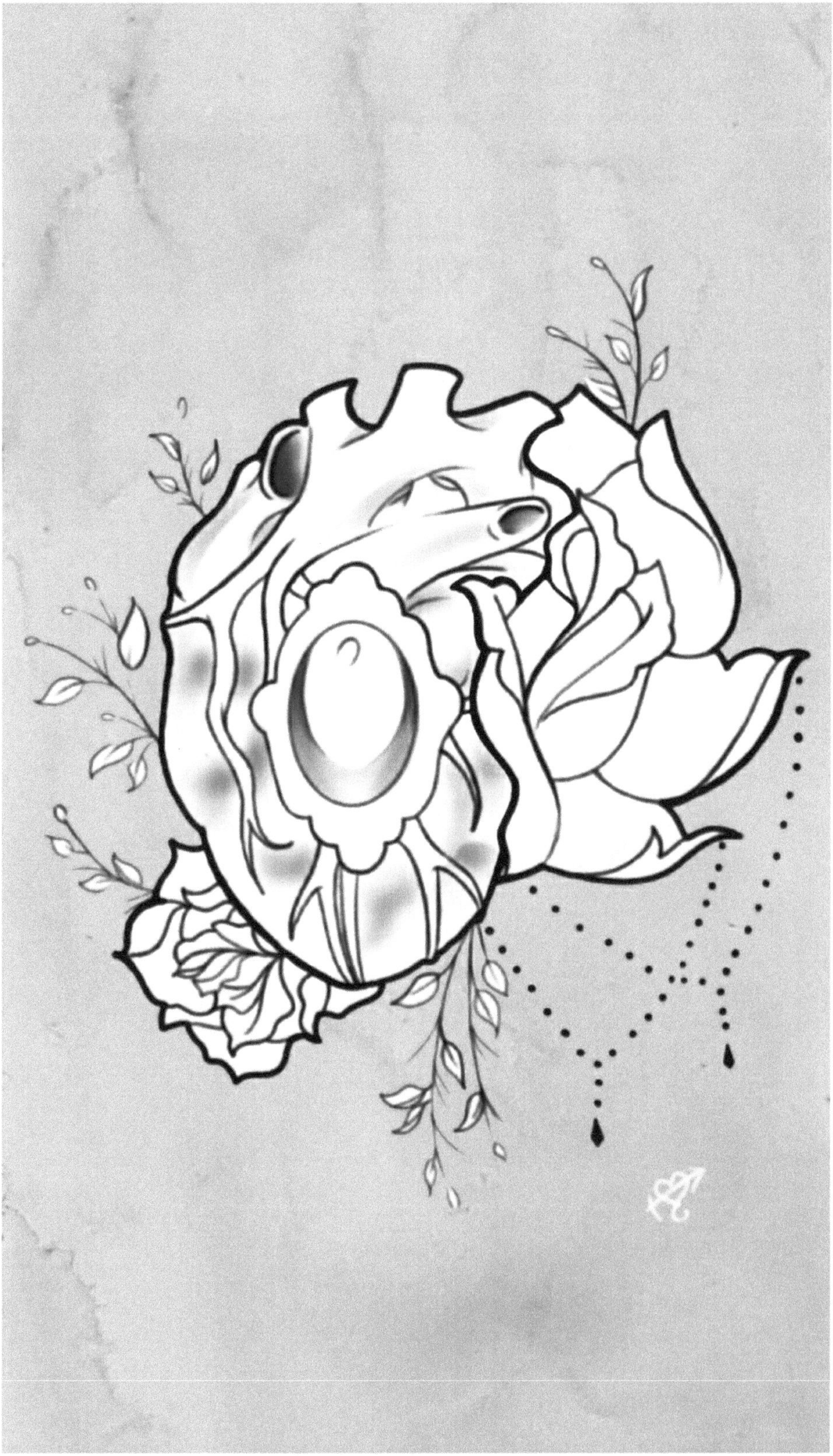

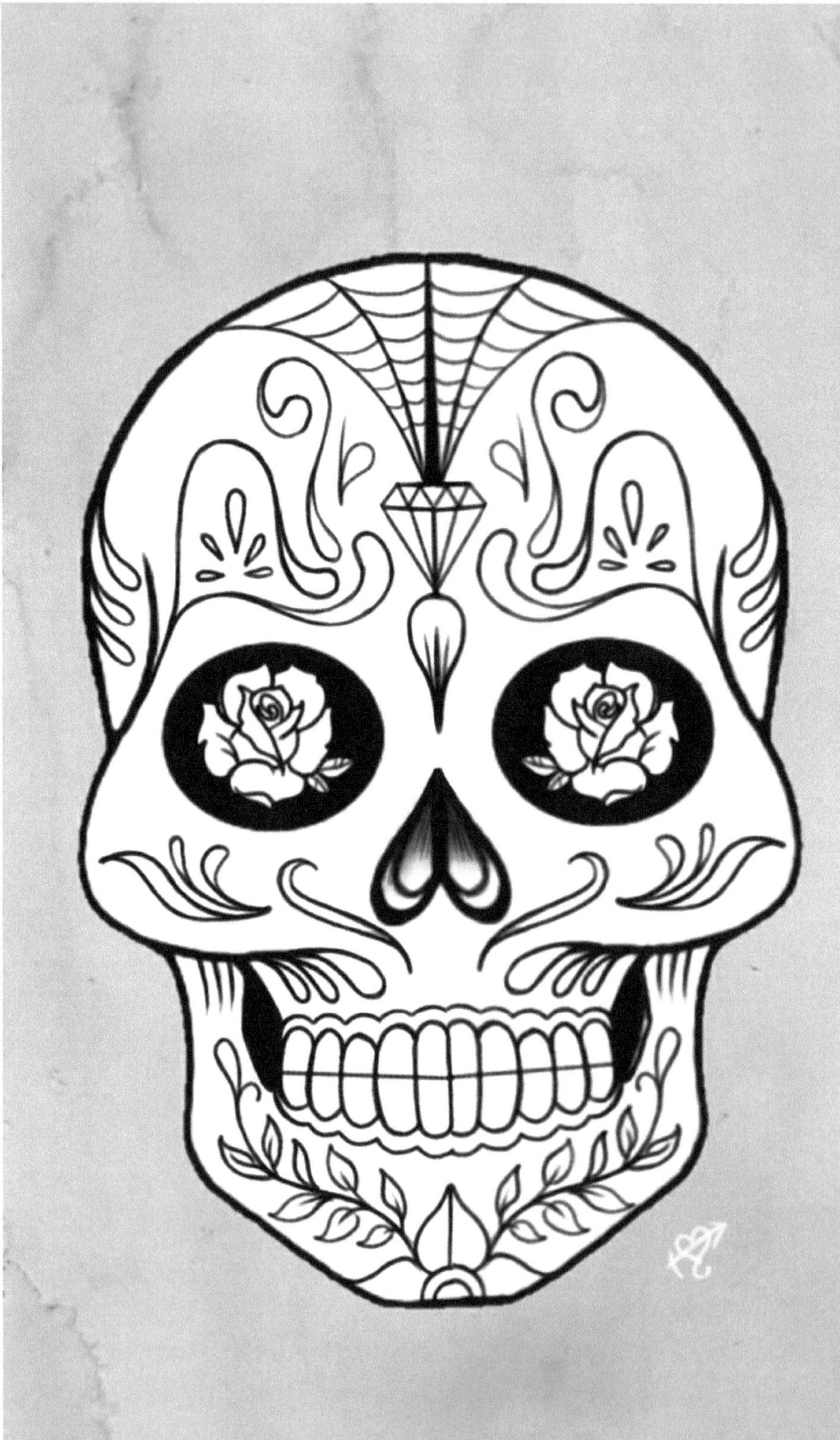

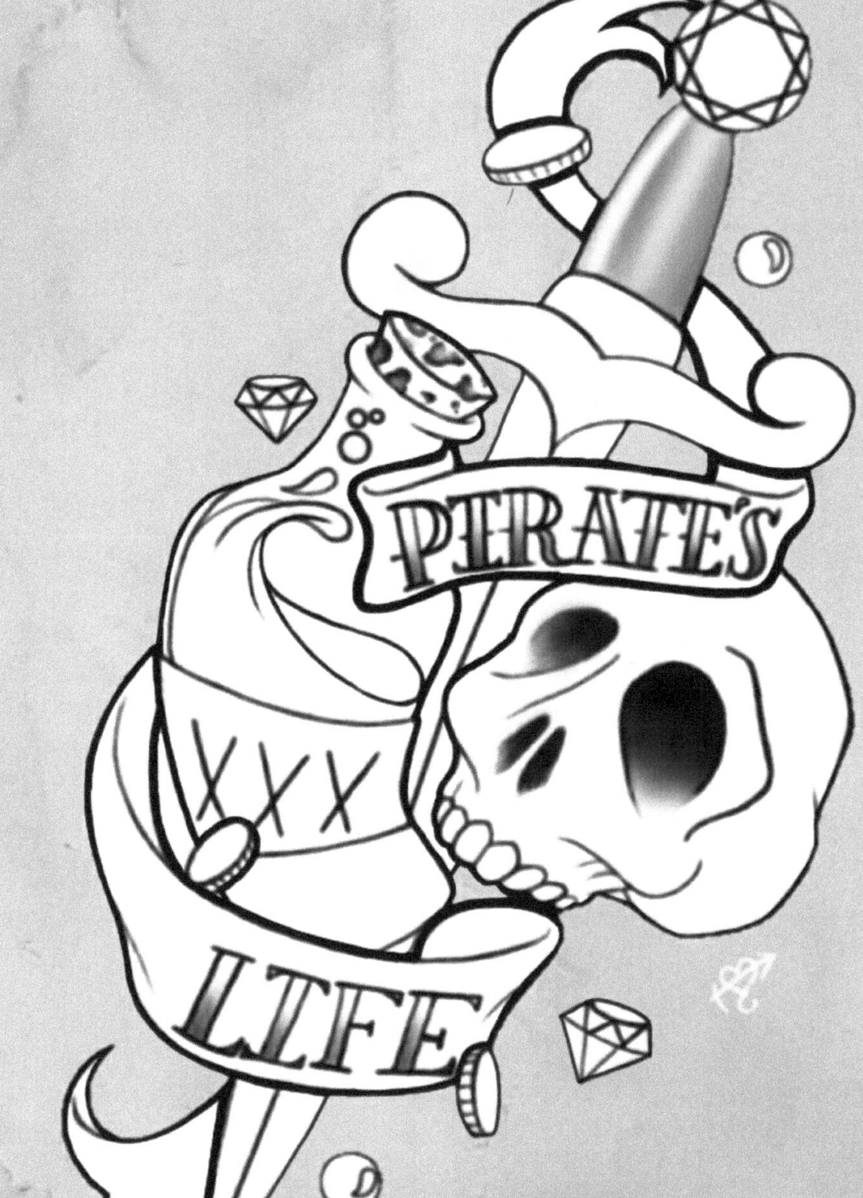
PIRATE'S
XXX
LIFE

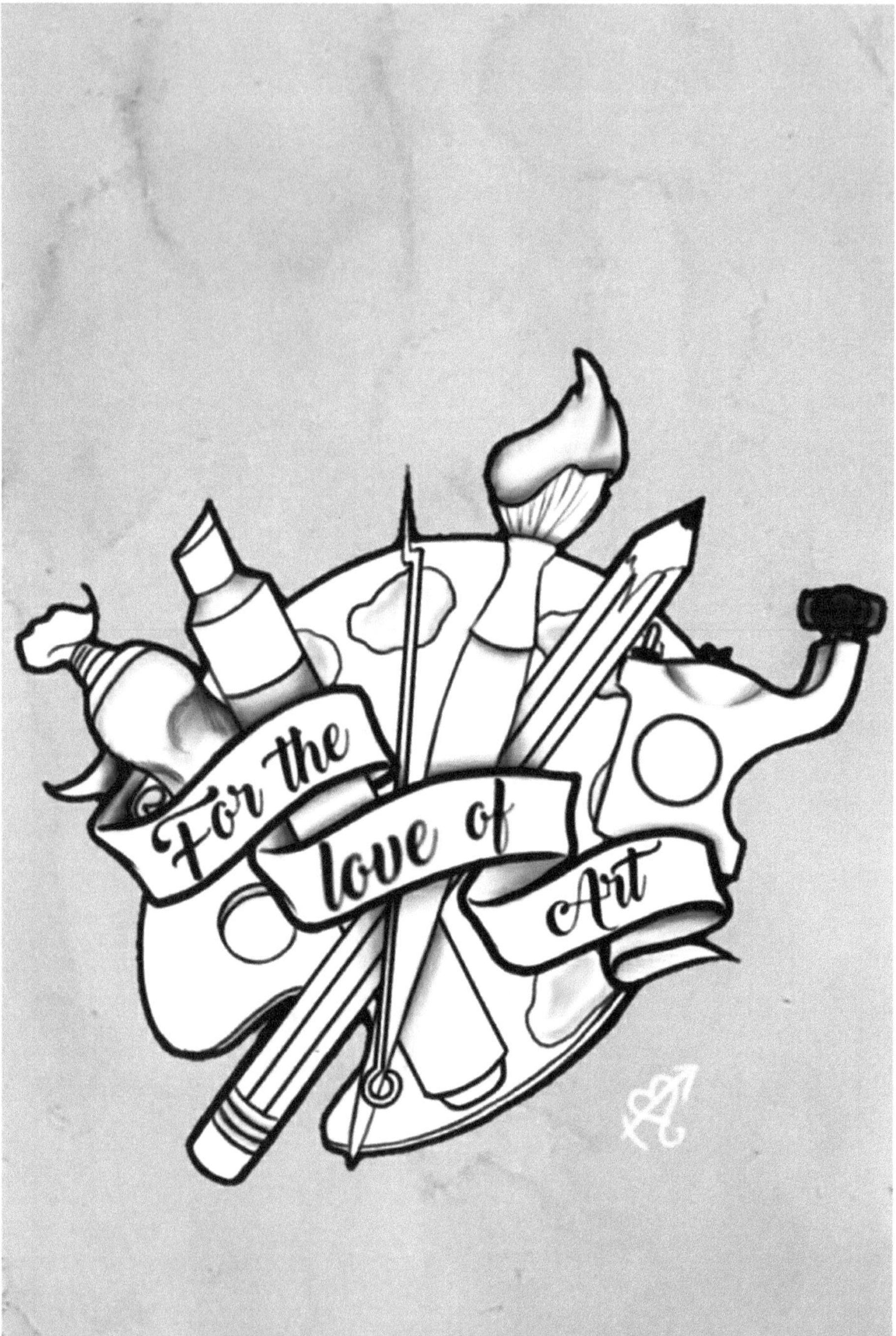
For the
love of
Art

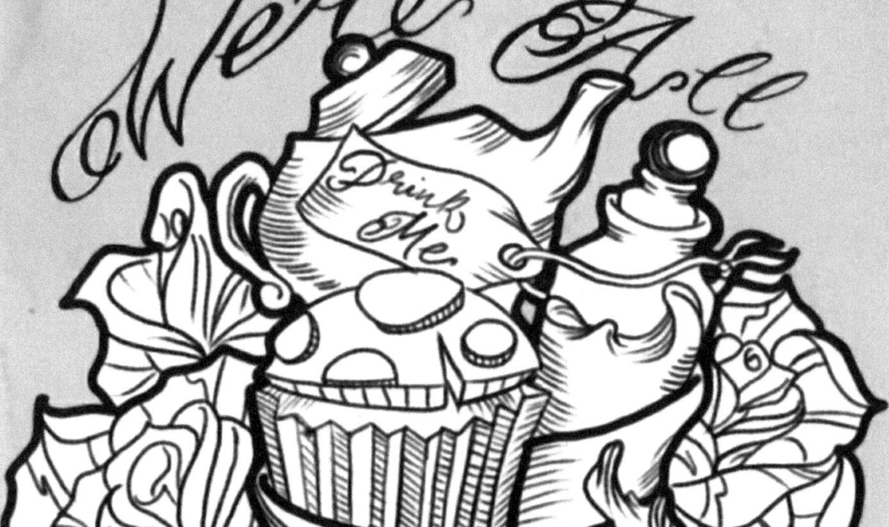
We're All
Drink Me
Mad Here

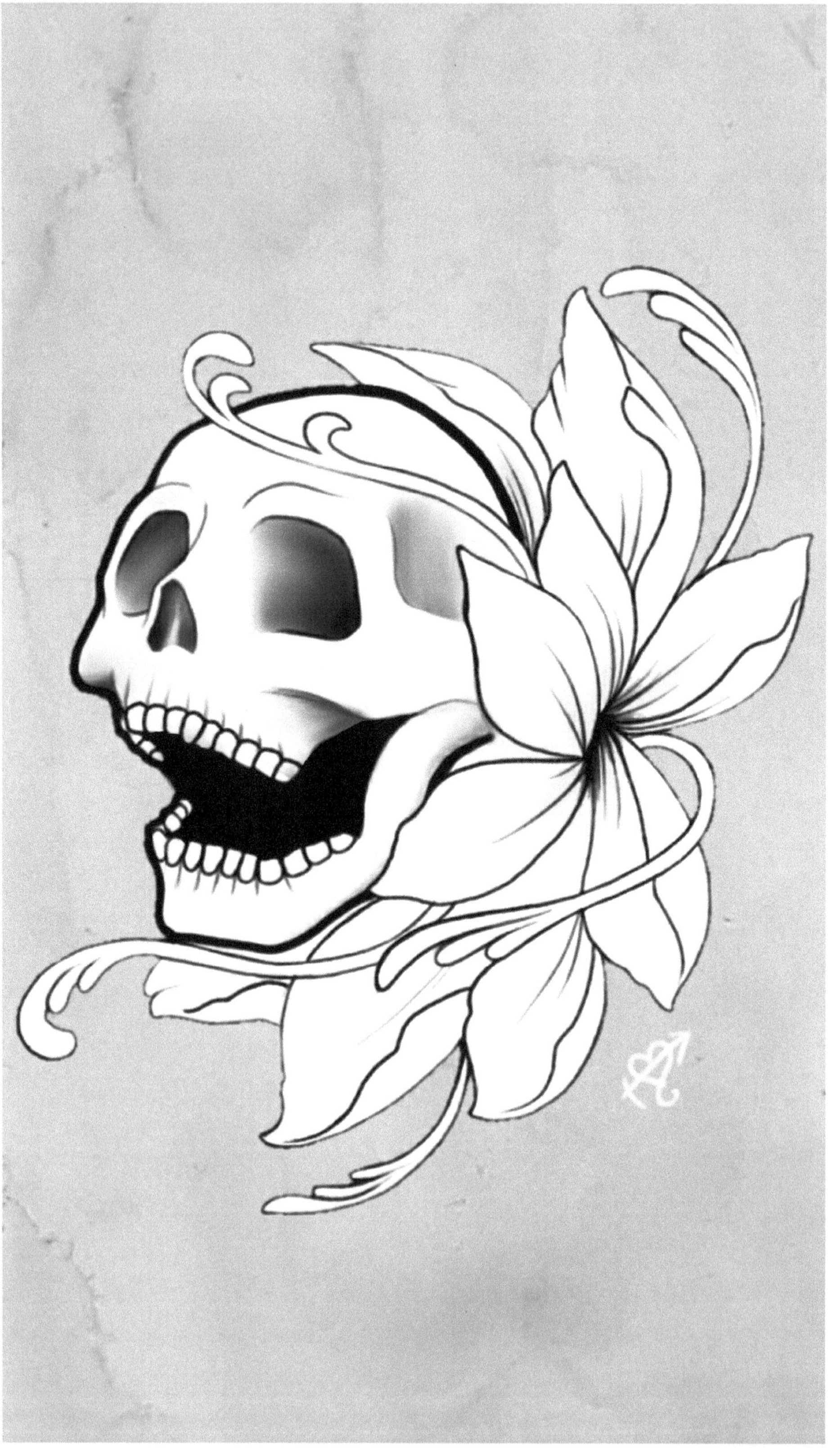

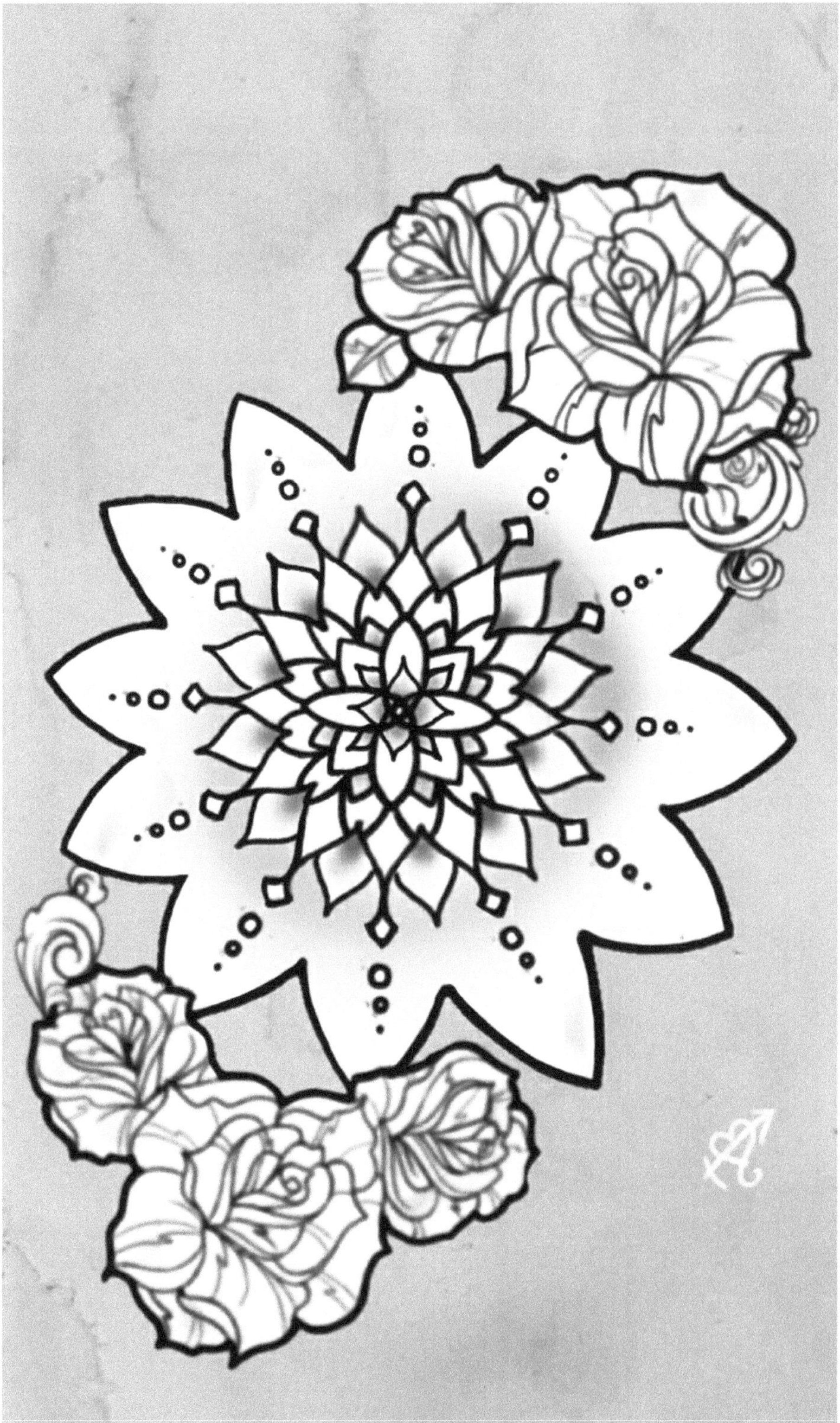

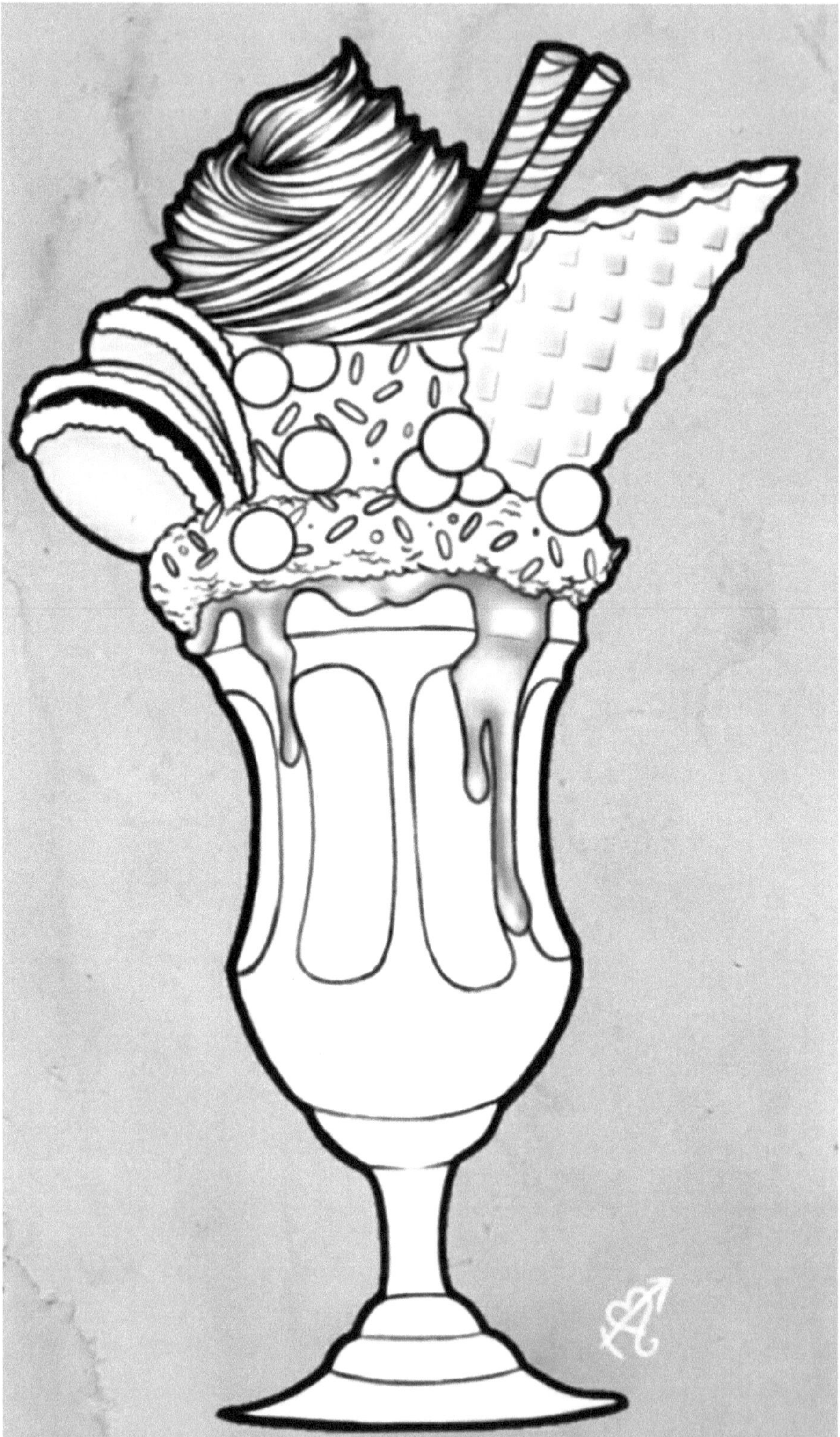

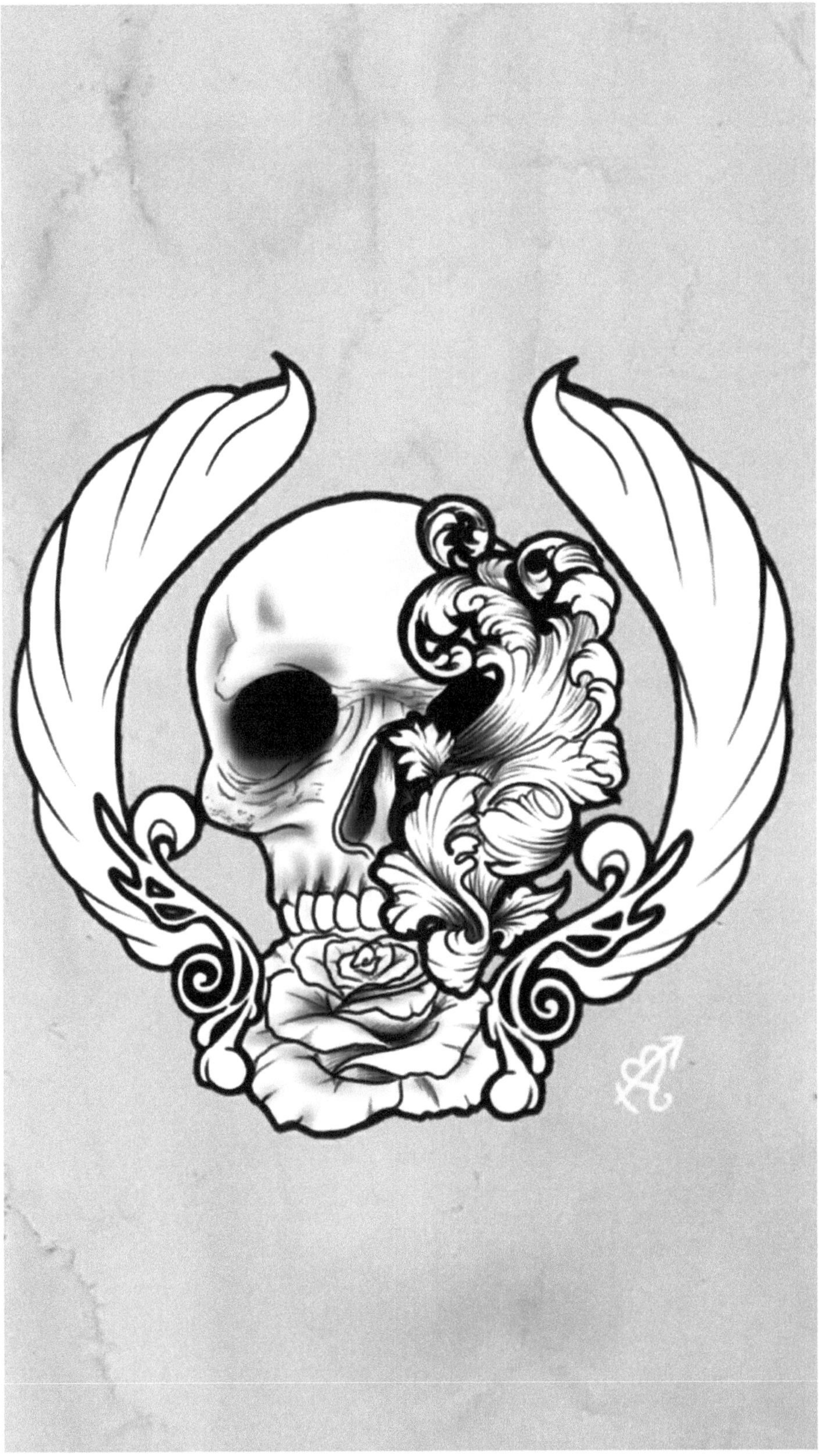

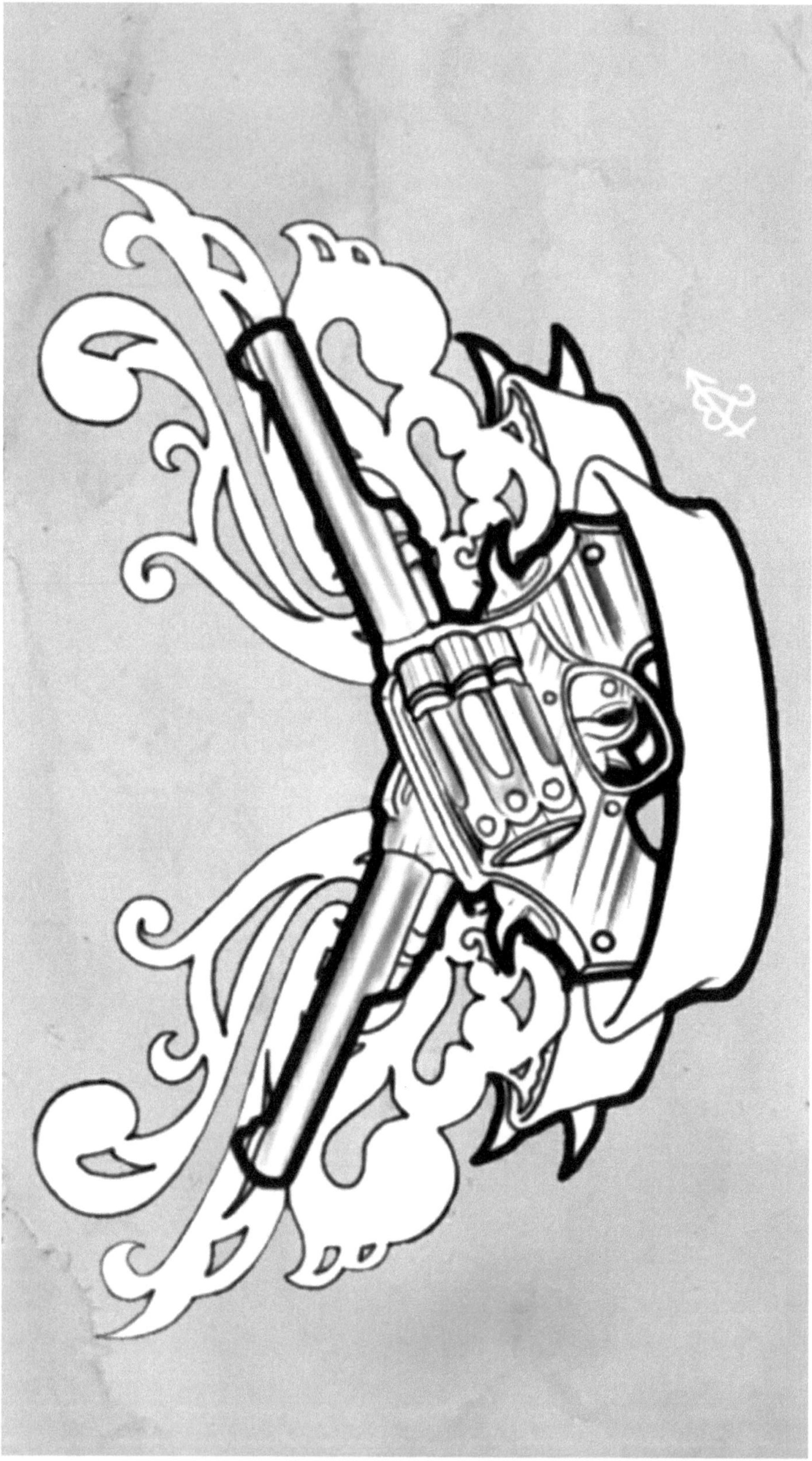

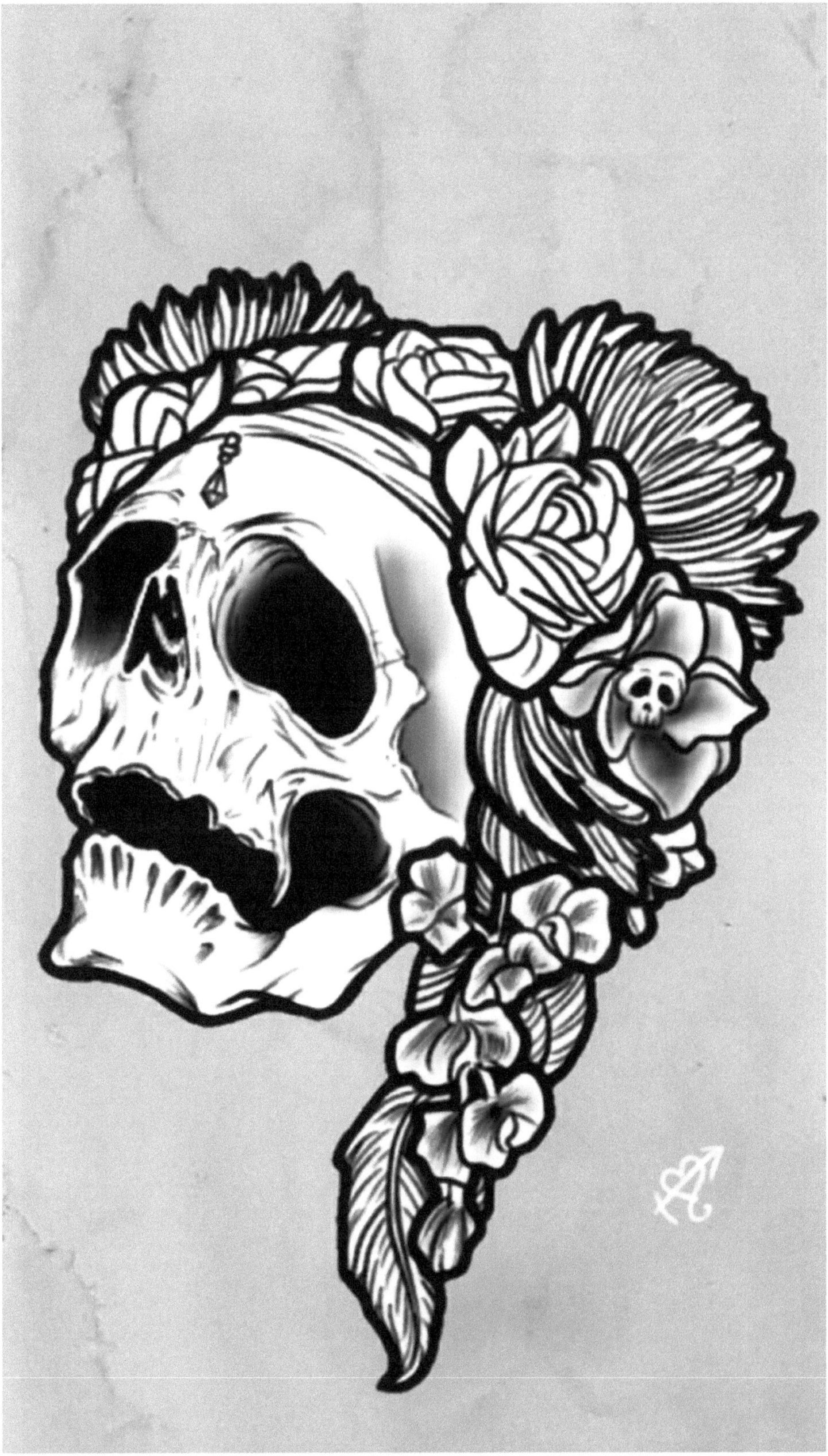

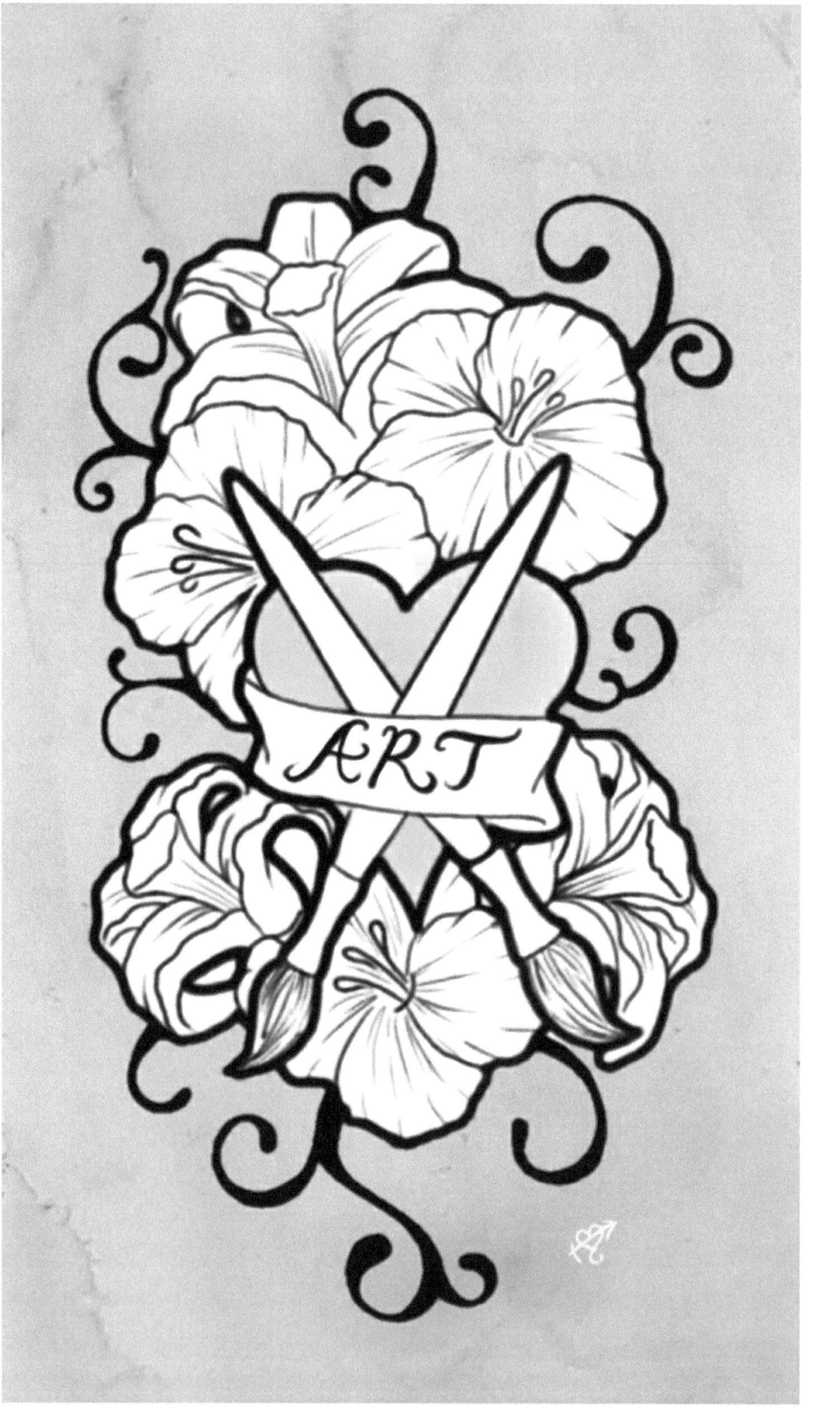
ART

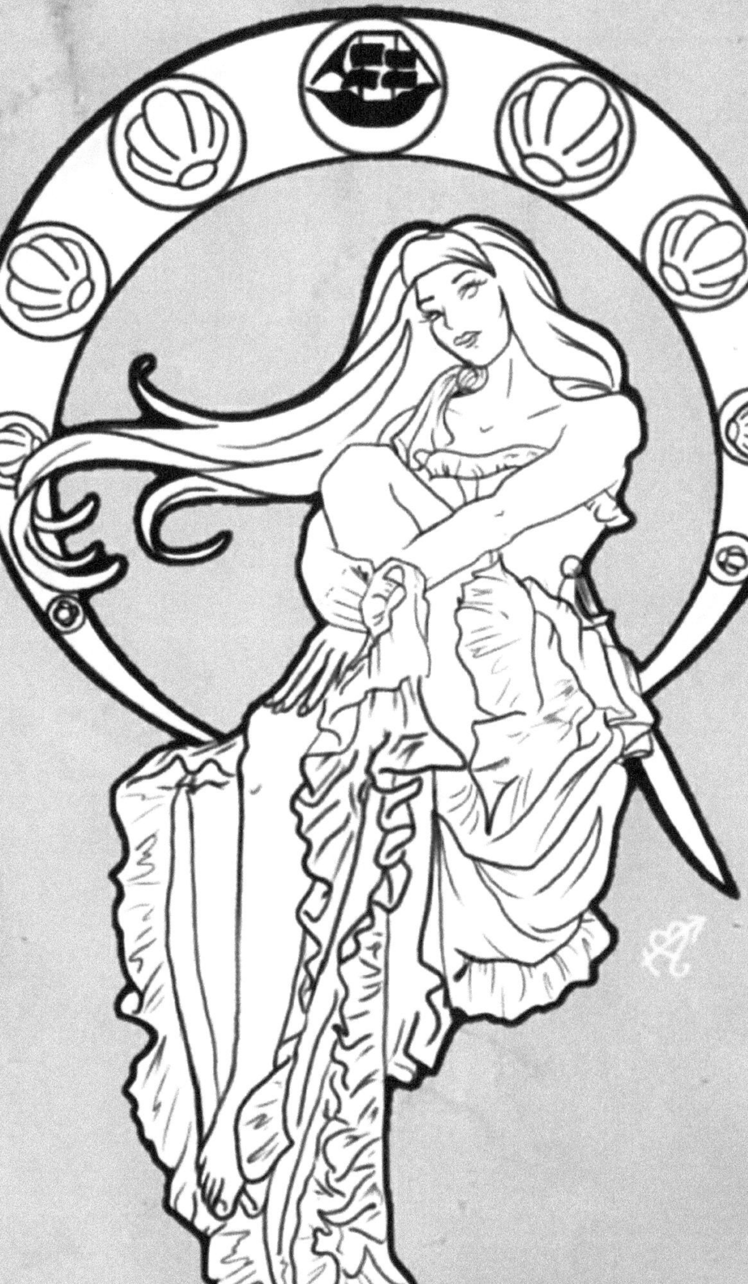

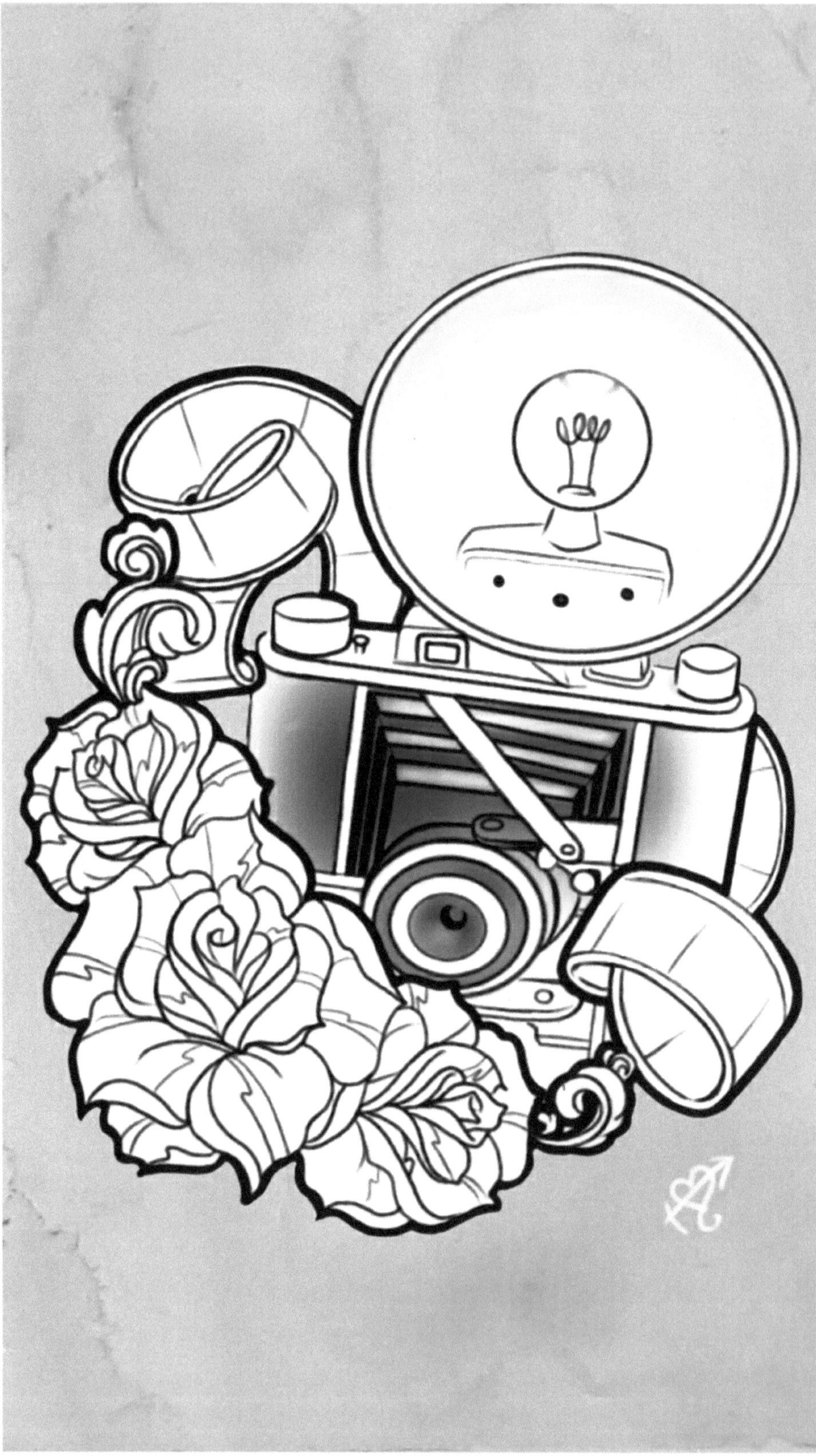

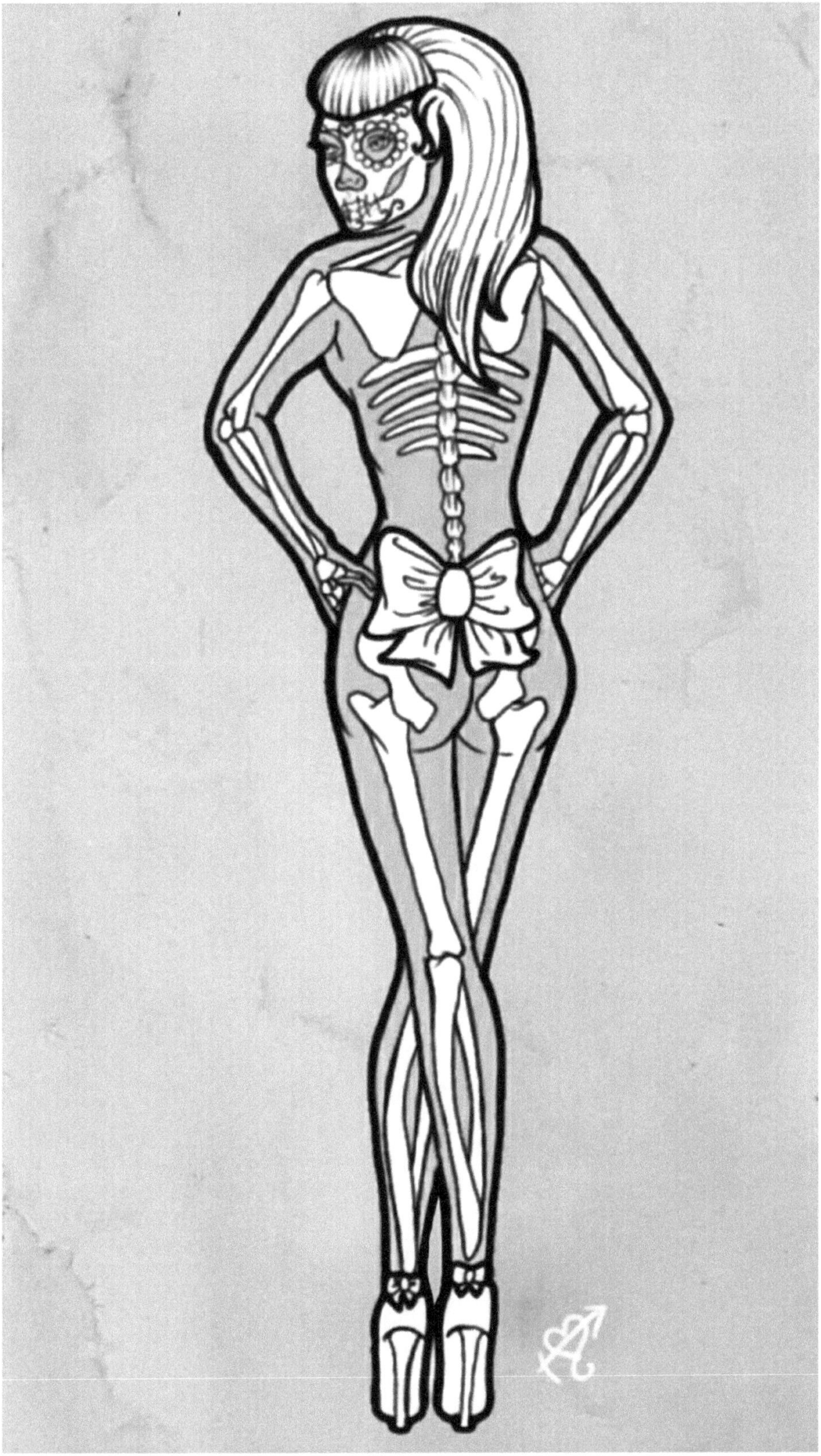

www.ingramcontent.com/pod-product-compliance
Lightning Source LLC
Chambersburg PA
CBHW041142180526
45159CB00002BB/708
* 9 7 8 0 6 9 2 8 0 5 7 5 6 *